Staying After School

Staying After School

19 Students (for Real!) Have the Next
What-if Word on Remarkable Fictional
Teachers and Their Often Challenging Classes

Robert Eidelberg

To order additional copies of this book, contact:
Xlibris
1-888-795-4274
www.Xlibris.com
Orders@Xlibris.com
767069

Contents

Author Robert Eidelberg:
"Books With a Built-In Teacher"

In addition to **Staying After School: 19 Students (for Real!) Have the Next What-if Word on Remarkable Fictional Teachers and Their Often Challenging Classes**, the following books by educator and author Robert Eidelberg are available through amazon.com, bn.com, xlibris.com, and authorhouse.com.

So You Think You Might Like to Teach: 29 Fictional Teachers (for Real!) Model How to Become and Remain a Successful Teacher

Good Thinking: A Self-Improvement Approach to Getting Your Mind to Go from "Huh?" to "Hmm" to "Aha!"

Stanza-Phobia: A Self-Improvement Approach to Bridging Any Disconnect Between You and Poetry by Understanding Just One Poem (Yes, One!) and Winding Up Not Only Learning the Process Involved but Coming to Love at Least a Few More Poems (and Maybe Poetry Itself)

Detectives: Stories for Thinking, Solving, and Writing

Playing Detective: A Self-Improvement Approach to Becoming a More Mindful Thinker, Reader, and Writer By Solving Mysteries

Julio: A Brooklyn Boy Plays Detective to Find His Missing Father (with John Carter)

Introduction

Yo, my reader…

…and now that I have your immediate attention (and am that close to losing your respect with my word play on the "Hi, teach!" opening to Bel Kaufman's famous school novel *UP THE DOWN STAIRCASE*), please stay with me a bit longer so that I can tell you how *STAYING AFTER SCHOOL* came to be the place where nineteen real students (they're in college, after all!) take a look at remarkable fictional teachers and their often challenging classes.

For the 2016 – 2017 academic year at The City University of New York's Hunter College campus, I created and then taught a "special topics" English Department literature study and creative writing course I first called "School's In." However, I soon caught the cuteness of my ways and changed the title to "The Teacher and Student in Literature."

Inspired by my 2013 book *SO YOU THINK YOU MIGHT LIKE TO TEACH: 29 Fictional Teachers (for Real!) Model How to Become and Remain a Successful Teacher,* my elective course on "The Teacher and Student in Literature" was initially advertised for the fall semester as open to qualified Hunter College undergraduates and soon filled up with nineteen students ranging from upper freshmen to upper seniors; in its second semester in the spring, a total of twelve students included a graduate student majoring in Secondary Education in Physics and a foreign exchange language student from Spain. Across the academic year's total of thirty-one students, the most popular major was "undeclared," but English, sociology, psychology, and pre-nursing were also right up there.

Described as a cultural and literary look at schools, classrooms, and their very real, though fictional, inhabitants, "The Teacher and Student in Literature" probably appealed to potential students (I'm not being modest here) mostly because of this unambiguous line at the very end of its lengthy college catalog description: "There are no exams as such."

Probably less clear and compelling were the words (I'll paraphrase) that preceded that "no exams as such" marketing and recruitment line: "Blah...blah...blah, this is a reading, literature study, thinking, talking, and writing course (heavy on creative non-academic writing) with a variety and range of projects and presentations about the sociology of schooling as revealed in the personal and professional lives of remarkable fictional teachers and their students." Fortunately, that miasma of meaning did not frighten too many students away from my English Department elective.

STAYING AFTER SCHOOL, the book that follows that course, is a sort-of-but-not-quite successor to *SO YOU THINK YOU MIGHT LIKE TO TEACH*. Which is to say that *STAYING AFTER SCHOOL* is my second book about what makes good teaching tangible and true learning lasting – but in an original form with a host of collaborators: a "class act" assortment of "what-if" wondering by college students who figuratively "stayed after school" to have the next imaginative word on classes and classrooms both fictional and actual. After all their "reading, thinking, and talking" about school novels and movies, here are their "creative extrapolations" from the works of such well-known authors and directors as Bel Kaufman, Evan Hunter, Frances Gray Patton, Leo Rosten, and Richard Brooks.

Robert Eidelberg

Dedicated to remarkable teachers and challenging students everywhere – and in honor of Max Cohen, my "mensh" of an "Uncle Mac," who truly cared and always asked about the courses I had created, the students I was teaching, and the book I was currently working on; his good and long life taught kindness

19 Contributing What-if Writers (for Real!)

Daniel Garcia-Munoz Garcia

Christine Gargano

Taylor Fatima

Jamal Stovall

Evan Wezik

Krenare Celaj

Lilly Lin

Messay Kassi

Jack Link

Valeria Diaz

Raquel Levy

Gabriel Carela

Marianne Feliciano

Kalleen Marte

Rachel Steinman

Georgette Kadianakis

Christen Schuchardt

Claudia Ng

Robert Barber

And a sincere and succinct thank you to Arlene Kase for her editorial insights (and parenthetical remarks)

1

It's a Jungle In There (and Never Mind That the Classroom Blackboard Is Now White and Soft)

I f you are interested in the profession of teaching as a possible calling or simply intrigued by what goes into good instruction and real learning (and that "odd couple" relationship of challenging student and remarkable teacher), this book with its unusual origins might be the book for you.

STAYING AFTER SCHOOL is neither a sequel nor a prequel to my 2013 book *SO YOU THINK YOU MIGHT LIKE TO TEACH*, though it does share some of that earlier work's connections to famous set-in-school novels and films. Let's call this book a companion piece that wants to be instructive about public school education by collaboratively showcasing the "what-if" writing of a diverse group of students on the Hunter College campus of the City University of New York.

Incited by a variety of creative writing assignments in my Hunter English Department course "The Teacher and Student in Literature," these mostly undergraduate students have been wondering out loud and then writing imaginatively about both actual and fictional schools they've "attended" recently. What these nineteen students have to say about "education" – that teaching and learning dynamic – is part "telling it like it is," part "showing you how it was," and a whole lot of creating how it might be if some famous novels and films that take place in schools were put on pause and then imaginatively forwarded.

Figuratively speaking, these nineteen college students have "stayed after school" on the elementary, secondary, and adult-ed levels in order to offer serious and sometimes seriously comic what-if exploration of what they believe actually happens (or should be made to happen) on both sides of the twenty-first-century's teacher's desk when there is a kind of chemistry between a remarkable teacher and a challenging student. Although my voice and the voices of several renowned authors of school fiction can be heard throughout the nine chapters of *STAYING AFTER SCHOOL*, this book is truly these college students' book. (For real!)

For example (and our first "teaching moment"), **Staying After School** student ***Robert Barber*** reminisces about the science education juvenile fiction series *THE MAGIC SCHOOL BUS* created by author Joanna Cole:

> *THE MAGIC SCHOOL BUS science picture books are one of the most vivid memories from my childhood. They were the one series I enjoyed reading the most, over and over again. And the Public Broadcasting television series based on the books was one of my favorite shows to watch as a child. (My elementary school science teacher actually used to show us many of the episodes and relate them to her lessons – and I loved it!)*

> *The truly remarkable teacher in THE MAGIC SCHOOL BUS books was Miss Frizzle (commonly referred to as "The Friz"). Miss Frizzle is a third-grade science teacher who uses*

*rather unusual methods (marvelous trips on a magic school
bus!) to teach her children (she thinks of her students as
her children) about the world of science. Miss Frizzle has a
bubbly personality, always tells jokes, and stays light-hearted
with her students. Above all, she cares not only about them
but also for them.*

*What makes Miss Frizzle a "remarkable" teacher is her
personality and her teaching methods, her flair and her
pedagogical style. Because Miss Frizzle treats her students
like they are her own children, she tries to protect them the
best she can. In the book "The Magic School Bus at the
Waterworks," Miss Frizzle constantly reminds the children
to be safe. She says, "Watch out for the rocks, children" as
they are heading over a waterfall, and she tells them to "stay
together, children" as they drop into the river. In "The Magic
School Bus Lost in the Solar System" Miss Frizzle reminds
her children to put on their special sun goggles as they head
closer to the sun.*

*Always on the lookout for teaching moments, Miss Frizzle is
determined that her children learn something on every one
of her fun trips. When in the book "The Magic School Bus in
the Time of the Dinosaurs" her class magically travels back
in time to see dinosaurs first hand, Miss Frizzle points out
that "coelophysis have excellent teeth for eating meat; their
teeth have saw edges, like steak knives."*

*Also, Miss Frizzle is constantly challenging her students to do
some learning on their own: whenever they ask their teacher
questions, Miss Frizzle refrains from giving direct answers,
forcing the children to investigate and solve problems*

themselves. When the class gets lost in the solar system in the picture book of that name (with Miss Frizzle herself getting trapped in an asteroid belt!), her students are forced to work together and problem-solve to save their beloved teacher. (I actually think that this was a science lesson planned on her part, but this is not confirmed in the book.)

Miss Frizzle is such a remarkable teacher: she adds spice to learning and makes acquiring knowledge engaging and easy. Many people, myself included, wish we had a Miss Frizzle as a teacher growing up because she got her class out of the mundane classroom and took the students on fun intellectual adventures: she wants her class to go out, work, and learn – it's okay to fail, but get back up and work twice as hard.

The remarkable Miss Frizzle represents to me the hard-work and never-give-up attitude of America. As Miss Frizzle says: "Take chances, make mistakes, and get messy."

And now, first up in adult school fiction for extended analysis and **Staying After School** what-if creative extrapolation are the "fraternal twins" of an artistic endeavor collectively known as *BLACKBOARD JUNGLE.*

Before there was the sensational 1955 juvenile delinquency movie *BLACKBOARD JUNGLE* directed by Richard Brooks, there was another kind of "picture" of high school life in urban America. That "picture" took the form of an in-your-face illustration on the cover of crime writer Evan Hunter's 1954 paperback novel *THE BLACKBOARD JUNGLE* (with the "the").

Never depicted in the many editions of the novel quite this way again, here is what Evan Hunter's potential reader first sees and then

tries to make sense of (before he decides to buy this paperback or
"pocket book" that can literally fit into his back pants pocket):

- in the bottom right foreground is a provocatively buxom open-jacketed white teenage girl (even though the school is all boys) with a closed book in one hand and the other hand saucily on her hip;
- standing next to the girl is a bow-tied and suited young-looking high school teacher who appears to be explaining something to her from an open book he is holding;
- over the teacher's right shoulder in the center background but fading into the distance is a sportily dressed black teenage boy looking straight out at the reader;
- down from the teacher in the bottom left foreground is a polo-shirted white teenage boy looming out at the reader with a piercing look in his eyes and an open switchblade knife in his left hand;
- over them all, marquee-style, in large all uppercase letters is the title of the novel and underneath it in script-like italic writing the words "*A novel of juvenile delinquents.*"

A sight for shocked eyes? And some questions for consideration:

- What sense did the first "readers" of the novel's cover art make of life in 1950's America and of its urban high schools and their student bodies of rock 'n' rollers?
- How did these same viewers of the cover art of a book they were considering buying (at a 1954 cost of 35 cents) explain what that alluring female was doing outside the novel's all-boys vocational high school?
- What's with all these different individuals juxtaposed in a kind of artistic collage under the book's pointed title in bold

block letters – *THE BLACKBOARD JUNGLE* – and its italic description as *"A novel of juvenile delinquents"*?

- And, last question, how much of a role did overt or unconscious racism play in so many potential readers' insisting, when questioned, that the opened switchblade knife was definitely in the hand of the single black male student depicted on the cover?

When potential readers of *THE BLACKBOARD JUNGLE* become actual readers they soon meet a black high school student who accuses his white teacher of being a racist. The teacher counters, adamantly, that he is not prejudiced against black people and that absolutely no prejudice of any kind affects his pedagogical persona and teaching style.

The teacher is Richard (Rick) Dadier, the major character in the narrative arc of the novel and a boyish-looking high school English teacher with a French last name. (Not that the linguistic origin of his surname matters to his students since, initially, Rick's most disrespectful students insist on calling him "Daddy-oh" while his somewhat less disrespectful students settle for "teach" and "chief.")

As *THE BLACKBOARD JUNGLE* opens, Rick is beginning his first year as a regularly appointed teacher in a fictional – but very real – New York City vocational high school – the decidedly all-boys North Manual Trades. Like the several other vocational high schools under the aegis of the then "Board of Education" of the city of New York, North Manual Trades has as its foundational purpose to prepare graduating seniors to join the work force in such practical "trades" (job categories) as plumber, woodworker, carpenter – any "handy" occupation that involves making or fixing things ("manual" means "using your hands").

However, certain North Manual Trades "veterans" (mostly jaded teachers who have put in a lot of years) are, in fact, quite prejudiced – without discriminating: they consider *all* vocational high school students "garbage" and see their "teaching" job as nothing more than to "keep the lid on" – on the "garbage can" filled with male adolescents who are not mentally able to or just won't learn either such basic academic skills like reading, writing, and math or the specific practical skills that a particular vocational secondary school has been established to specialize in toward gainful employment.

During the course of the novel, Rick spends his first year of teaching "fumbling" toward connecting with his students, in particular Gregory Miller, a non-achieving but intelligent (as well as street-smart) black student (who will be in both Rick's daily attendance-taking homeroom class and one of his five assigned English classes). Miller, as he is referred to in the novel, is actually caught by Rick on Day One smoking a cigarette, against school rules, in the school's lavatory. First impressions are negative on both "sides," with Rick assuming that Miller is nothing more than a troublemaker and Miller concluding that Rick is an out-and-out racist with particular prejudice against black people.

Also on Day One of the new school year, Rick, in the right place at the right time, prevents the rape by a North Manual Trades student of a newly assigned and alluringly dressed female teacher, Lois Hammond. In the 1954 novel, the physical assault and attempted rape occur in one of the school's deserted stairwells; in the Hollywood film version of the novel, released only just one year after the book's publication (and currently available on YouTube), the sexual assault and Rick's subsequent mano a mano fight with the student take place in the school's deserted library.

It's instructive for readers and viewers of the "fraternal twin" BLACKBOARD JUNGLE to speculate on how these two particular venues for the near-rape of a teacher inside a public high school send somewhat different messages to the American public about the safety of teachers and students in America's institutions of public education. Perhaps the venue with the more ironic overtones is that of the unattended school library, a setting normally associated with the humane power of knowledge, reason and order.

Nevertheless, in both versions of *BLACKBOARD JUINGLE*, Rick becomes a "hero" to the school's faculty and staff but a "villain" and "traitor" to most of the school's students because their fellow student gets reported to the police by the school's principal.

Staying After School student ***Marianne Feliciano*** sees new teacher Tansy Culver (Miss Tansy to her class in Richard Peck's 2004 young adult novel *THE TEACHER'S FUNERAL*) as a small town version of big-city Rick Dadier in Tansy's heroic role of replacement teacher in a one-room schoolhouse that contains her school-phobic younger brother Russell. The novel begins with the death of the sole "schoolmarm" of many years literally days before the new school year is about to start or as we are told in Russell's voice and in a classic opening sentence for a school novel: "If your teacher has to die, August isn't a bad time of year for it."

Russell's immediate reaction to his sister's agreeing to take the job is that his sister is no hero who has saved the town's school year but a traitor to her very own brother and his several friends. As ***Marianne Feliciano*** puts it:

> *Although this relationship of teacher and student has a somewhat different dynamic in THE TEACHER'S FUNERAL because Tansy and Russell are also siblings, Tansy actually agrees to become the school's sole teacher so her younger brother will learn the importance of intelligence in the working world and finally graduate from eighth grade; for their part, Russell and his friends will go on to master the course of study (and more) because they sincerely want Russell's sister to succeed when she is later officially observed teaching their class. In short, learning and teaching need mutual caring and understanding for a true follow-through.*

In a creative writing assignment to choose fictional students encountered in "The Teacher and Student in Literature" course and

have these students present an annual "Teacher of the Year" award to
any of the course's fictional teachers, **Staying After School** students
Jack Link and *Daniel Garcia-Munoz Garcia* each selected the
same "odd couple" pair of teacher and student. (Please note that as
with *all* writing by professional authors and by college what-if writers
quoted in this book, their pieces are graphically represented in script-
like *italics*.)

In both of their testimonials, *Daniel Garcia-Munoz Garcia* and
Jack Link extrapolate from author Evan Hunter's plot and character
development to have "hero" Rick Dadier win "The Teacher of the Year"
award at the end of Rick's inaugural year of teaching at North Manual
Trades. And both have Gregory Miller, the "featured" black student in
Rick's starting-out year of teaching, present the prestigious award to
Rick. Just as Rick continually "mused" about teaching and learning
in Hunter's novel, the two **Staying After School** what-if writers
have Miller philosophize on how neither being a teacher nor being a
high school student in the 1950's is "easy" and on how he as a black
adolescent came to change his mind about Rick as a teacher and as a
person.

*Gregory Miller's "Teacher of the Year Award" testimonial
speech honoring Rick Dadier as imagined by Daniel Garcia-
Munoz Garcia:*

> *It's my privilege, and an honor for all the students here at
> North Manual Trades High School, to give this award to our
> teach, Mr. Rick Dadier, for teachin' us that English can be
> useful for us as well as for bein' so patient with us (we know
> we're sometimes not easy!). For all of this, we give you this
> award, 'cause we dunno another better way to thank you. By
> the way, the story 'bout the dragon was awesome, an' there is
> nothin' I enjoyed more than the fun tape recorder lesson you*

did (it even got us to think seriously about the different races, and religions, and groups that make up our class). I don't want to be too long, 'cause I ain't no good at talkin', but I just wanted to say, in the name of my classmates – "Thanks, Chief!"

Gregory Miller's "Teacher of the Year Award" testimonial speech honoring Rick Dadier as imagined by Jack Link:

Well, won't you look at all this, Chief? I never thought I'd be up here saying this, but congratulations on your award. I remember the first day we met – in the school bathroom: you came in putting on the tough guy act with me and I could read right through it, but what I didn't know that day was that you were just doing your job and striving to be your best for us. As you know, Mr. Dadier, we didn't always get along in the classroom and I hope you can put those days behind us because after this year I truly respect you as a colleague and human being.

I know it got chaotic at times in our class, but that's just how we feel about learning and sometimes it wasn't you but us. As a first-year teacher, I think you did a fine job at trying to teach us and motivate us a class, but one recommendation for your next class is to make your lessons more relatable to us since we don't always know what you're getting at; imagine yourself in our shoes.

I could see that you were truly frustrated up there some days in the front of the room with us, and I understand even more now why you felt that way: it was simply because you wanted to teach us, you wanted to get through to us. You see, Mr.

Dadier, what you're doing here at North Manual Trades isn't an easy thing, nor is it easy for us to come here and try to learn. I commend you for that reason, of being here for us, not giving up on us and trying to get through to us with your heart, and you have my respect, Mr. Dadier. Hopefully, we'll have a class together next year, Teach, and you and I will manage the class together this time.

However, **Taylor Fatima**, a fellow **Staying After School** student and what-if writer has chosen, instead, to have the new principal of Manual Trades High School, Mr. Small, single out for special mention Rick Dadier's first-year accomplishments *not* in a "Teacher of the Year" award but as part of his own "you-made-it" address to the faculty at the school's traditional end-of-school-year assembly.

Since Principal Small, an ironic name in the novel if ever there was one, has also just survived *his* first year in that top administrative and supervisory high school position, **Taylor Fatima** thought it natural to have her version of Principal Small (larger-than-life!) not so subtly contrive in his personal tribute to Rick Dadier to also give himself a couple of "I-also-made-it" pats on the back.

Address to the faculty of Manual Trades High School from Principal Small at the end of the school year as extrapolated by Taylor Fatima:

Welcome everyone! I meant it when I said at the start of the school year in my first address as the new principal of North Manual Trades that I intend to make this school one of the best damned schools in the urban vocational education system – a school where knowledge and practicality will always be welcome. We've had a pretty good year, with a few bumps along the way – but, overall, pretty good. Hey, Rome

wasn't built in a day, and it is going to take some time before
everything runs smoothly. But we are off to a good start.

As your new principal, I had faith in all you teachers that in
the event that a situation might arise you would all be more
than equipped to handle it – and you were. I appreciate my
staff equally, but I'd like to bring attention to just one of you
right now – Mr. Richard Dadier. Mr. Dadier has successfully
completed his first year as a vocational high school English
teacher at North Manual Trades High School. From his first
day in the building, Rick has been working in the trenches
and I'd like to commend him for that. Each term we will
watch this school grow better and better and that's due to our
lovely faculty. Everyone, give yourself a round of applause –
and I'll see you all next term.

And many, many fictional years later, after staying at North Manual
Trades for his entire teaching career, Rick Dadier, according to the
what-if whim of several **Staying After School** students, decides to
put down the chalk and retire. What will Rick have to say about how he
answered the "calling" of teaching? Does he think that teaching is about
being a "hero"? How and from whom do "newbie" teachers learn to be
a success with their students? Why is it such a "battle" to be effective
and make a difference? Does teaching even matter?

Veteran teacher Rick Dadier's end-of-career retirement
speech as imagined by the first of three what-if writers,
starting with Lilly Lin:

Teaching at North Manual Trades is an experience I will
never forget. It allowed me to fully understand that being a
teacher is one of those careers where you learn along with the

students, where mentor and mentee are mutually inclusive. Every student is different but all of them have the potential to want to learn, to escape society's prejudices against them, and to get something out of the high school experience. Teaching is not about being a hero – and the pay is not glamorous either, but what makes it worthwhile is when you make that first breakthrough to your students. The hushed silence and wide-eyed stares that escalate to excited chatter and enthusiasm and, most importantly, a curiosity, a yearning to learn more. It is this very reason that I have continued to be a teacher till this day. Thank you!

Veteran teacher Rick Dadier's end-of-career retirement speech as imagined by what-if writer Kalleen Marte:

Good evening, everyone. First I want to thank you all for being here tonight. I know I have not been the easiest of co-workers but you have all managed to become very dear to me. It has been an honor working beside you through the years, to have learned from you and alongside you. When I first started teaching here at North Manual Trades High School, I said that I would not become a hero and, by God, as most people would say I blew that out of the water on the very first day. And that action to help Miss Hammond was a perfect indicator of what my teaching career would be – unexpected.

At first, it seemed unexpected in the most terrible ways. I found that my students were unwilling to learn. I could not fathom how it was possible for someone to not want to learn or care to learn. But as that first year went by I realized that it was much deeper than them just not caring or wanting to learn. And, I told myself that if I reached just one of them, just one, my career would have been made, all the trouble would have been worth it, because as you know we didn't always have the nicest students here. But, at last, I reached one student and to this day that is still one of the biggest accomplishments of my life: to know that I have changed someone's life, that I have given them the tools to try, to persist and succeed – and then watch them do it is an inexplicable thing.

I almost gave up on trying to reach them, but I'm glad I didn't because, while unexpected, it was in the most wonderful of ways. Through the years there have been many more Gregory Millers for me, but there have also been those that slipped through the cracks. Yet, I would never in a million years think to trade my career. I have given this school and my students the best years of my life and the best I could give, and I hope, no, I know that it has mattered, that I have mattered and for that I am ever grateful.

In an "it takes courage" retirement speech what-if writer Evan Wezik has veteran teacher Rick Dadier look back on all the times he went "once more unto the breach":

(After a round of applause) Thank you. Thank you very much. I'm deeply honored to be standing before you today. Lord knows there were days where it seemed like this would never happen. As I reflect on my times in these halls, I can't help but think what a journey's it's been for me here, over these past years. You know, over the course of this my last year as a teacher I've been finding myself contemplating the day I came for my job interview.

As I sat and spoke with Mr. Stanley (the English chair who recommended to the then principal of North Manual

Trades that I be hired) he accused me of being a rather "soft spoken" individual. In order to counter the claim I recited words of a man who we should all be familiar with, William Shakespeare: "Once more unto the breach, dear friends, once more...."

And in case anyone's wondering, that's "Henry the Fifth" (not "Henry the Fourth," as Chair Stanley purposely misstated during my job interview to see how I would handle correcting a possible future boss in his area of expertise). It's a speech that King Henry gives in order to instill courage into his men. Courage. You know, when I took this teaching job, I initially felt a long list of things: excitement, nervousness, pride, ambition. But after my first day I realized I needed something more. Something to get me through the very threshold of the school: courage.

Many of you know how trying this job can be. It's not a job anyone can do. There have even been those who've attempted to do it only to quit and walk away from this school and its students. So I ask you, why do we do it? Why do we come into this place every day and stress ourselves out to try and teach students who, more times than not, show such resentment towards us?

I think of another quote from "Henry the Fifth," one where King Henry is addressing his troops before battle. You see, the king's men were feeling discouraged because they were facing impossible odds. It was a fight that they did not feel confident they could win. They lacked courage. Yet Henry gives a rousing speech about how they will put up a fight worthy of remembrance. He doesn't sugarcoat or downplay it. He tells them it will be a fight that will scar them, yet those scars will show the world the heroism they displayed: "Then will he strip his sleeve and show scars, and say, 'These wounds I had on Crispin's day.'"

So I ask you again, why do we do it? Why do we go into the breach every day and do battle against a force that is so opposed to us? Well, I can't answer for you; you all have your reasons. And if you don't, then I implore you to consider why you are here. There must be a reason for you to put yourself through this struggle. But what I can do is to beseech you to take pride in the scars you bear doing it.

Oh, some of you may not have physical scars – and consider yourself lucky 'cause there are those of us who do. But we all face the same mental and emotional anguish this job has to offer, and that can have a lasting effect on us. Yet despite all of that, we chose to do what very few have the courage to do. And we should take pride in that.

Unlike King Henry, I'm not for giving long speeches so I'll leave you with this: Amongst these students are those that can be reached. There are those who can be taught. And there are those who will contribute to society. To reach them is a battle, but it's a battle we can win. I thank you all for years of friendship and camaraderie. It will not be something I forget. I wish you all nothing but the best. Fight on. Thank you all.

And, finally, to close out this chapter, **Staying After School** student and what-if writer ***Marianne Feliciano*** has the nephew of now grown-up student Gregory Miller pay tribute to Rick Dadier on the

occasion of Rick's retiring from teaching, fully nineteen years after Rick
first taught his uncle Gregory:

> *I ain't never wrote anything like this or had to make a speech
> before but I'm happy I get to do this for Daddy-oh, or should
> I say Mr. Dadier? He's finally leavin' after nineteen years
> teaching in North Manual Trades Vocational High.*

> *When I was first sent here, I remember my uncle talkin' my ear
> off about Mr. Dadier, and I didn't believe one word he said.
> He'd say, "Listen here, Chief, ain't nobody a better teacher
> than Richard Dadier. Show him respect or he'll demand it!"
> Of course, this wasn't my first plan for a school and Dadier sure
> wasn't my first choice for a teacher. But after the second week
> of school, when he read that dragon story and we all decided
> to finally listen, he taught us that everyone needed a crutch.*

> *If he ain't here breakin' up fights, he makin' sure he's
> everybody's crutch. He didn't treat us like less, he treated us
> smart and actually cared about us. I ain't the only one feelin'
> this way; anyone who had Mr. Dadier knows he's hard –
> but a good teacher. If it wasn't for him, we wouldn't have
> graduated, we wouldn't know why we need good English
> for a trade. If it weren't for him, we wouldn't have a good
> Christmas show to go to every year.*

> *My uncle tried to keep me on a good path, but ain't nobody
> else made me believe in me than him, so it was hard. But
> Mr. Dadier was the best crutch the class could ask for. You
> taught my uncle there was better – and you taught me to be
> better. I ain't never goin' to forget you. You a goddam hero!*

2

A School System That Is a "Tribute to Our Communities and to Our Faith in American Youth"

In 1955, a fast year after its publication as a "shocking" novel about American juvenile delinquency in our nation's urban schools, a filming of *THE BLACKBOARD JUNGLE* was released by a major but yet nervous Hollywood studio – Metro-Goldwyn-Mayer (MGM) – as a black and white movie. Since there was, of course, color cinematography in the year 1955, it's instructive if you plan on seeing the film (which is available on YouTube) to try to come up with some tentative reasons why its director, Richard Brooks, purposely – and purposefully – didn't shoot it in color.

Minus the *"THE"* of the novel's title, this cinematic version of America's epidemic of "juvenile delinquency" was instead entitled the more-in-your-face *BLACKBOARD JUNGLE*. Practically all of its scenes were shot *not* on location in a gritty New York City but at MGM's west coast Hollywood studios. (The name of the movie's urban vocational high school was bizarrely changed to the nonsensical "North Manual

High School," the "Trades" being presumably dropped so as not to upset any of the many trades people in the United States who might be potential viewers.)

One extended sequence of scenes, however, *was* shot on location – at what looks like the campus of a seemingly all-white American middle class suburban high school with individual scenes highlighting eager-to-learn students actively using all the latest technology in fully equipped labs and classrooms and gentlemanly playing sports on well-tended athletic fields.

However, these scenes were *additional* to the original film *BLACKBOARD JUNGLE* and were shot only *after* filming had already been declared completed ("in the can"). What accounts for this additional filming being done after the film was officially announced as "ready to be released"? The apparent answer to that question is that MGM had become so anxious about the film's negative image of America's young people and of the nation's urban public schools that certain key members of the cast and crew were called back to film this very particular and purposeful sequence of scenes set on the campus of a suburban academic high school that *never appears* in the novel.

For most of this sequence, Rick Dadier's newly written and rehearsed dialogue characterizes him as in awe of everything he sees on a private tour by his teachers' college mentor of what appears to be an all-white school. The entire suburban academic experience is in such stark contrast to Rick's working days at his ethnically diverse urban vocational high school and its "culture" of delinquency that Rick seriously considers leaving North Manual Trades for a regular teaching position at any school far removed physically and psychically from the problems and troubles of America's inner cities.

Inserted into *BLACKBOARD JUNGLE* under the pressure of persuasion before even half the movie is over, these scenes speak to the rising fear that MGM and its chain of movie houses had that the American movie-going public (this is at the height of the Cold War with Russian communism) would find Richard Brook's original filming of the novel anti-American – an outrage to the history and cultural values of democratic America – and that negative word of mouth would kill it at America's box offices from coast to coast and from North to South. Even with these additional scenes, several pro-American European countries, concerned that cold war Communist propaganda might use *BLACKBOARD JUNGLE* to prove that the United States was falling apart, refused distribution of the film within their borders.

And domestically in the United States, the city of Boston kept the sound totally off for the opening minutes of the film for future showings of *BLACKBOARD JUNGLE* after the overwhelmingly adolescent audience at the film's Boston premiere jumped up from their seats to enthusiastically dance in the aisles to the soundtrack of the hit rock 'n' roll song "Rock Around the Clock" (sung by the pre-Elvis Presley group Bill Haley and His Comets). Meanwhile, the film's extended opening credits rolled on and on in complete silence.

But even these opening credits were *not the first visuals* any American or foreign audience for *BLACKBOARD JUNGLE* saw; instead, viewers (dancing up a storm or not) got to read and think about (like a novel's cover art) this five-paragraph statement of explanation:

We, in the United States, are fortunate to have a school system that is a tribute to our communities and to our faith in American youth.

Today we are concerned with juvenile delinquency – its causes, and its effects. We are especially concerned when this delinquency boils over into our schools.

The scenes and incidents depicted here are fictional.

However, we believe that public awareness is a first step toward a remedy for any problem.

> *It is in this spirit and with this faith that BLACKBOARD*
> *JUNGLE was produced.*

After pondering the very existence of such a statement preceding the start of a modern American movie, **Staying After School** students analyzed the statement for what it was saying, implying, hiding, and fabricating (in the sense of lying about); then ten what-if writers rewrote the statement – first individually and then collectively – to convey what they believed was truly behind and beneath this "incredible" statement's words.

The following verbal collage or "fabrication" – in the sense of a composite statement – reflects the thinking and language choices of **Krenare Celaj, Christine Gargano, Valeria Diaz, Taylor Fatima, Kalleen Marte, Lilly Lin, Jack Link, and Daniel Garcia-Munoz Garcia.** They collectively give the opening statement of *BLACKBOARD JUNGLE* a good old-fashioned schoolhouse-caning punishment.

> *We in this country are fortunate enough to be made up of*
> *many diverse communities that co-exist together, and our*
> *national public school system appears to be a tribute to our*
> *country as a whole and to our faith in our youth and their*
> *varied personalities and talents; however, in reality, the only*
> *people we Americans really care about are the white young*
> *people who live in our suburbs.*
>
> *As a human race, we are faced with challenges in our lives –*
> *some harder than others – and as long as we live, we will*
> *need people to have faith in our youth with their multiple*
> *personalities and talents and to be there for them, supporting*
> *them with a passion. Often, the only adults really there to guide*
> *what is the future of our country are our nation's teachers.*

Now, more than ever, we need teachers who inspire their pupils and mirror the qualities that are essential to being a part of society in and out of school. Nevertheless, this country does not always live up to these expectations in some of its schools and, as a result, juvenile delinquency – its causes and its effects – is ripe in them.

This is no joke; it is a real problem that cannot be narrow-mindedly perceived because teenage delinquency can boil over into the real world. People need to see that; we cannot turn our backs on it. These issues require our immediate attention because our youth is our future.

This situation in our schools is, in fact, a by-product of our society's ills and of the loss of societal values that we have tried but have failed to maintain. In these mostly urban schools (particularly our inner-city vocational schools), students have a poor foundation for learning – but if we teach our youth that racism, class-ism, ageism, and sexism are wrong in schools, they will reflect that in their communities. That's the sociology of American public schooling in BLACKBOARD JUNGLE.

Although some of the scenes you are about to see are alarming, we believe that our nation's students have the ability to learn and flourish. Kids are not all bad: there is always a story behind a face; everyone has their own personal struggle and obstacles that they are trying to overcome. We must have teachers who care about them and are willing to help them, teachers who will pour love into their students and provide them with the teaching that they may not be receiving at home.

*This movie you are about to see shows various aspects of our
country's culture: you will see various dynamics of school and
of family life, as well as several coming of age stories. Each
individual has a story.*

*The incidents depicted in this film (exemplifying the dynamics
of what goes on in a particular school, especially the
relationship between teachers and their students) are fictional
and exaggerated; the scenes that are presented are but one
side of the problem and might be interpreted as an attempt on
the part of us – the makers of the film – to absolve ourselves
of responsibility, to transfer the blame elsewhere; however, to
some degree, these scenes do contain a kernel of truth that we
seek to expose to our audiences, as many of these incidents
actually happen in many schools throughout our country.*

*Although public awareness may be the first step toward a
remedy for any problem, awareness alone is useless if these
next steps are not outlined and followed: we must persevere
against the sentiment that there will never be any change
in this problem; in fact, we believe that patience and a firm
understanding of a teacher's mission in connecting with
students is an essential first step to changing our outlook and
then taking action by speaking out. This will be an ongoing
arduous process that will bring about equality.*

*It is in this spirit and with this faith that the film you are
about to see has been produced. In a world full of hate,
we want not only the people of our nation to know what is
going on within our educational system but also the world in
general so that all of us can contribute as far as possible to
improving the system.*

> *Our film is a cautionary tale of what could happen to our nation's youth if we do not put in the time and the funding that our public school system needs in order to provide safe, fair, and positive learning environments for all our youth.*

The truth about the film *BLACKBOARD JUNGLE* and its original "viewer beware" warning? Not the whole truth, of course, but perhaps a hefty piece of it.

What if?

3

A What-if Help Wanted Ad: "Not Too Feeble" Teacher Needed for Two-Room English Village Schoolhouse

I n the very same year, 1955, that *BLACKBOARD JUNGLE* – a film depicting urban America – opened across the United States, the British author known as "Miss Read" published a novel in Great Britain in which a sudden and unexpected teacher vacancy needs to be filled in an old-fashioned two-room (but not red-painted, that's American) village schoolhouse.

"Miss Read" is the penname of Dora Saint, who wrote a whole series of popular novels on a vanishing village life in rural Great Britain. In "The New Teacher" chapter of her 1955 novel *VILLAGE SCHOOL*, Saint tells us pretty much everything we would want to know about the dynamic of teaching and learning in an English village's perhaps soon-to-be extinct school "system." *Except* the actual wording of its help wanted ad for a desperately needed new teacher, which is to say that what is missing from Saint's novel are the position's particulars about teaching and learning, the job's specifications, and any of its required professional qualifications.

A sudden vacancy has occurred in the early grades at the two-room schoolhouse of Fairacre School in the village of Fairacre, England – and Mr. Partridge, the village vicar, needs to find and hire a qualified replacement. Consequently, Mr. Partridge puts an "advert" (as the British abbreviate the word "advertisement") in two national educational publications and schedules it to run for several weeks.

But what exactly does Mr. Partridge's advert say that will entice sufficient qualified candidates for the job? Saint herself does not say, but can readers of "The New Teacher" chapter of *VILLAGE SCHOOL* confidently draw their own conclusions based on the village's longstanding but threatened commitment to local control of elementary schooling?

Not surprisingly, given the nature of the job and whatever the job specifications listed, Vicar Partridge's advert elicits an interested response from only three women, all of whom are interviewed, not in the schoolhouse, but in the dining room of the vicarage ("a large Georgian house of warm red brick, standing among sloping lawns and looking out upon two fine cedar trees"). The interviews are conducted by the vicar along with the three other school managers: Miss Parr, Colonel Wesley, and Mr. Roberts.

Miss Parr, who has never set foot in the school, is "an old lady of nearly eighty" who is "fabulously wealthy" and says she is fond of children ("even those modern ones that do nothing but eat gum").

Colonel Wesley, also nearing his eightieth birthday, "calls in to see the children on occasions, and is, of course, invited to all school functions, as are all the managers." The third manager, Mr. Roberts, far from eighty, is the youngest school manager and having himself attended elementary and grammar schools "has a first-hand knowledge of elementary education and he, along with the vicar, has a close understanding of the practical needs of the school in their care."

Saint's thirteen-page *VILLAGE SCHOOL* chapter on "The New Teacher" contains each of the three interviews (with a Mrs. Davis, a Miss Winter, and a Miss Gray), which were all held on the same "Thursday afternoon, late in January."

From "The New Teacher" chapter of *VILLAGE SCHOOL* by Dora Saint ("Miss Read"):

"I think we should begin," announces the vicar. "The first applicant is Mrs. Davis, who has come from Kent." (He pauses and looks over his glasses.) "Er ... this lady has not had experience with infants, but would like to try. She has two children of her own, I believe."

"The second applicant," the vicar continues, "is a little older and has had experience in infant and junior schools in several towns in the Midlands. She is, at the moment, teaching in Wolverhampton. She could begin in March."

"What's the last like?" asks Mr. Roberts, stretching his long legs out under the table suddenly.

And the vicar answers, "A Miss Gray; very much younger, still in her twenties. She left the teaching profession last summer —"

"No disgrace, I hope?" says Miss Parr.

"Oh, no, indeed, no, no, no! Nothing of the sort," the vicar assures her hastily. "I understand she nursed her mother for some months, but is now free to take a post."

"Does she come from a distance?" asks the Colonel.

"Any chance of her living at home, I mean; or will she have to have digs in the village?"

At the conclusion of the three interviews, the vicar turns to the other school managers and asks them what they think of the last of the interviewees, Miss Gray:

"Well?"

"Best of the bunch," says Mr. Roberts, stretching his legs again.

"A very nice, ladylike gal," says Miss Parr approvingly.

"I liked her," says the Colonel.

Staying After School students analyzed all the scenes of the 13-page chapter to find, infer, and surmise what the specific job specifications might have been in the vicar's advertisement for "the new teacher." That analysis also included a close reading of an extended sequence of scenes toward the end of the chapter in which the chosen applicant (it turns out to be Miss Gray) visits and tours the village's sole boarding house where she will now live and take all her meals. During her tour, new teacher Miss Gray meets, briefly converses with, and forms some mixed opinions about the personality of the landlady, Mrs. Pratt.

As potential what-if writers, thirty-one **Staying After School** students not only searched all the interview scenes for direct and implied job specifications and professional qualifications but also probed beneath the surface of the boarding house scenes to discover more of Miss Gray's own personal character traits (revealed in her interactions with the chapter's other characters) that would have made her a good, or at least the best possible, choice for the position of "the new teacher."

Staying After School students were agreed that the most detailed, comprehensive, and insightful advert for the teaching and learning dynamic required in the village school of Fairacre, England, was the what-if advertisement that follows.

Help wanted advert created and placed by Valeria Diaz:

VILLAGE TEACHING POST AVAILABLE AT FAIRACRE ELEMENTARY SCHOOL

Fairacre elementary school is seeking a new teacher to begin teaching immediately. An ideal candidate would be one who has previous experience in working with young children and their challenges, preferably more than two years prior experience. Candidates should have referrals from all previous positions.

The position requires someone who resides at a close proximity to the school or is willing and able to move to Fairacre village and take up residence in our local boarding house.

This position involves working with kids of ages 5 to 10, so there is a level of discipline that needs to be asserted in order to assure that the highest levels of productivity and learning are achieved by both teacher and student. The post requires an individual who is comfortable and familiar with the position, has patience and care, and is not too feeble in character.

The position would best suit a sensible unmarried Christian young lady who has no other responsibilities to fulfill and who would naturally attend the Fairacre community's regular Sunday morning religious services.

This position is not to be taken lightly and there will be moments when it will prove to be difficult – but persistence and dedication are qualities that will come in handy when it is.

This position involves not only teaching the common subjects of English, grammar, and arithmetic, but, as well, handy skills that the boys and girls in the community will use in their everyday lives, such as needlework and musical skills.

Any qualified candidates are welcome to forward their information to the vicar, Mr. Partridge, who will then schedule interviews to be held at his home at a later date.

We conclude this chapter on hiring "the new teacher" with the following consensus prediction on the part of all thirty-one **Staying After School** students:

Miss Gray, the winning candidate for the position of "new teacher" at Fairacre village elementary school, will work out reasonably well since she was "not too feeble in character" for the demands of the job.

4

Classroom Management – and Other Mind Games That Teachers and Students Play

There are *GAMES PEOPLE PLAY* – or so declared the author Dr. Eric Berne in the title of his 1962 book on the psychology of relational power plays. And since teachers and students are people (I'm hearing you, but they are!) who usually and regularly relate weekdays from 9:00 am to 3:00 pm, there are a variety of mind games involving influence and control that both actual and fictional teachers and students play more than occasionally in the classroom.

For example, there is (named from the student's point of view) *Trip the Teacher* – a psychological game played in American author Frances Gray Patton's 1954 novel *GOOD MORNING, MISS DOVE* (same publication year as the American novel *THE BLACKBOARD JUNGLE*).

In the mind game of *Trip the Teacher*, Team Student is represented by the contentious elementary school pupil Angela Adams. Truth is, if Angela had not been so overly confident (downright cocky!) in her playing, she would have probably succeeded through her otherwise winning strategy.

Instead, Angela, "brash with the imminence of victory" makes a tactical error late in the game and winds up losing to Team Teacher, represented by "the terrible Miss Dove" – that "prim and proper" schoolmarm of Liberty Hill and that small town's epitome of gentility and wisdom.

What shall we call the game Miss Dove plays with pupil Angela Adams from the perspective of Team Teacher? Since game-naming is both a meaningful and a fun thing to do, how might "the terrible Miss Dove" – always "striving for a reputation for infallibility" – have named the game that she ultimately does win because her less-than-humble opponent Angela "saves the day for her"? Perhaps *Never Be a Pupil Who Pretends to Be Silly.*

Here is that part of the classroom scene early in the novel *GOOD MORNING, MISS DOVE* in which Angela Adams and Miss Dove take each other on:

> *Angela Adams – who had received in the Judgment Book a C for Contentious – had taught Miss Dove, indirectly, valuable lessons in the technique of classroom management…. In the show-offy way in which most children enjoy turning cartwheels or somersaults, Angela had enjoyed mental gymnastics. "Why" and "how" were her favorite words – tiresome words to a very young instructress who was striving for a reputation for infallibility – and when Angela uttered them she was apt to look smug as if she thought: "This time I'll trip the teacher!"*
>
> *Once, had she had the humility to leave well enough alone, she might have done just that.*

Miss Dove had been reading aloud from a book on the dietary habits of undomesticated animals. "Bears like honey," she read. "They are also fond of red ants which have a flavor similar to that of pickles."

Angela waved her hand. "How does he know, Miss Dove?" she had demanded. "How does the author know what ants taste like?"

The thirty-nine other children in the room had fixed their trusting eyes upon Miss Dove, waiting for her answer. Then Angela, herself, saved the day. Brash with the imminence of victory, she had pushed her advantage too far.

"Did he eat an ant to see?" she asked sarcastically. "Or did a bear tell him?"

The class had giggled. Ordinarily, Miss Dove frowned upon laughter, but this time it fell like music on her ear. She directed upon Angela her steady, solemn, scrutinizing gaze.

The child blushed. She folded her hands.

"Never pretend to be silly, Angela," Miss Dove said at last. She waited until a hush settled upon the room. Then she continued to read from the book.

As in a card game like poker, losing player Angela "folds" her hand(s); then first with widespread spectator giggling and later with a uniform hush, a room full of students officially certifies the remarkable Miss Dove's authoritative triumph over her challenging pupil.

Staying After School students were quick to find where "show-offy" Angela "pushed her advantage too far," making mind game moves that showed her to be a novice player who is smug, anything but humble, brash, pushy, demanding, and sarcastic. The pattern of Angela's poor tactics will be vividly clear to you if you take a second look at the above excerpt from *GOOD MORNING, MISS DOVE* and focus on *visualizing* the game – move by move by counter move – as the two combating teams employ a variety of tactics to advance their strategies and defend their positions against their opponent's plan of attack.

By the way, trying to visualize this particular game was something the makers of the 1955 Hollywood movie version of *GOOD MORNING, MISS DOVE* (same year as the film *BLACKBOARD JUNGLE*) *never attempted*. Although completely faithful to pretty much everything else in this early classroom scene in the Patton novel, Hollywood dropped the character of elementary school pupil Angela Adams entirely, as well as every single move and countermove of Angela's game with teacher Miss Dove. Too worried about 1950's American moviegoers' reactions to a young female student's challenge to a female teacher's intellectual authority? Maybe. In any case, good morning, Miss Dove – and goodbye, Angela Adams.

(Curious about the novel's answer to Angela's less-than-tasteful question? It's "yes" – and so did Miss Dove to verify the similarity of the flavor.)

A recent and truly "terrific" literary example of an iconic and "terrorizing" schoolmarm can be found in Robert Coover's short story "The Hanging of the Schoolmarm," which originally appeared in a fall 2016 issue of "The New Yorker" magazine. Set on the western frontier of 19th-century America, Coover's tale has his fictional schoolmarm winning ownership of a small town's saloon in an actual poker game and turning its card tables into school desks. Only because they "are awed by her refined and lofty character" do the fussing, cussing, hard-drinking men of the town initially let the schoolmarm have her pedagogical ways of wisdom. However, after getting their heads rapped too repeatedly with the schoolmarm's teaching tool (her long wooden ruler!), the men finally find that "it's too much for them. They form a jury and condemn the schoolmarm to be hanged for her cruel city ways."

For another instance of psychological combat and strategic power playing in literature, this time from the novel considered in Chapter 1, just recall *The Job Interview* mind game from *THE BLACKBOARD JUNGLE* that North Manual Trades English Chair Stanley plays with job candidate Rick Dadier. As contributing what-if writer **Evan Wezik** points out regarding which King Henry play it is that the famous Shakespearean line "Once more unto the breach, dear friends" appears in:

> *And in case anyone's wondering, that's "Henry the Fifth," not "Henry the Fourth," as Chair Stanley purposely misstated during my job interview to see how I would handle correcting a possible future boss in his area of expertise.*

Having concluded our admittedly limited consideration of the values, norms, and mores of small town America in *GOOD MORNING, MISS DOVE*, let's have some instructive fun with the "mental gymnastics" conjured up by several **Staying After School** students based on their own "original" psychological mind games – each "inspired by actual events" in their lives as middle school and high school students.

Taking their cue from *Trip the Teacher* and *Never Be a Pupil Who Pretends to Be Silly*, **Staying After School** students and what-if writers recall and then creatively embellish on several psychological mind games they know for a fact (and for real!) that students and teachers have always played.

THE GAME OF "OH, IT'S SOMEWHERE IN MY BAG!" by *Taylor Fatima*

> *I've witnessed this mind game take place dozens of times. Very popular in elementary, middle, and high school, it is not*

played on the college level because it is and always has been quite immature. I surely have never played this game myself; it's not in my character to play a fool and cause a scene – but it is quite entertaining to watch.

The game is called "Oh, it's somewhere in my bag!" and I've seen students spend up to twenty minutes searching and searching through their disorganized school bag for an assignment to magically appear, causing the class to converse and poke fun at the situation or watch intensely as their schoolmate looks for a non-existent item. I've also seen teachers who are less gullible/more strict give a zero on the spot to students who are not prepared, winning the game just as it got started.

Goals and Objectives for Team Student
- *get the teacher to forget about the lesson,*
- *waste class time,*
- *amuse the class,*
- *convince the teacher to let them hand the assignment in tomorrow because they must have "forgot" it at home.*

Goals and Objectives for Team Teacher
- *collect the assignment, or*
- *get the student to confess they did not do the assignment, and/or*
- *put an end to the game as soon as possible.*

Characteristics of Team Student
- *class clown/jokester/wit, or*
- *slacker (opposite of nerd), or*
- *liar, or*
- *disorganized student.*

Characteristics of Team Teacher
- *varies by individual teacher's persona,*
- *varies with days, months, years of teaching experience,*
- *dependent on teacher's "chemistry" with audience for – spectators at – the game (the rest of the students in the class).*

Overall Game Plan (Strategy) – and Individual Moves (Tactics) For Team Student
- *not give up,*
- *truly persuade the teacher that the assignment is in their possession and that any second now they will pull it out from the clutter of looseleaf papers sloppily thrown inside their bag,*
- *occasionally say "Give me one more minute, any second I'll find it for sure,"*
- *say something like "If you really need it today, I can call my mom to bring it from home" (knowing that the majority of teachers will not want this).*

Overall Game Plan (Strategy) — and Individual Moves (Tactics) For Team Teacher
- *not give up, which can backfire since this is also what Team Student wants,*
- *put an end to the game immediately.*

How Team Student Can Lose – and the Possible Consequences
- *teacher gives a zero on the spot, ending "the search" before it begins ("no late homework" policy),*
- *teacher enforces a "late homework with a lesser grade" rule, putting an end to the game (student can bring the assignment in tomorrow with a grade reduction),*

- *teacher punishes the student (calls parent; makes them stay after class or school; causes student to miss lunch or recess; assigns extra homework).*

How Team Teacher Can Lose – and the Possible Consequences
- *tells student to "just bring it in tomorrow" (which may result in the teacher being labeled as a "pushover" and earning the teacher less respect from all the spectators to the game).*

NAME OF THE GAME: "THE PEN DROP"
recreated for posterity by *Evan Wezik*

The objective of the game "The Pen Drop" is for the students (all equipped with several writing instruments such as a pen, pencil, or marker of some kind) to drop their writing utensils onto the floor to create disruptive sounds. The teacher will probably not realize what is going on at first. However, the more the students do this, the quicker the teacher will catch on to what is happening.

The goal of "The Pen Drop" is to disrupt the class by getting the teacher as annoyed as possible at the continuing dropping of pens. The game goes on until the teacher catches a student in the act of "the pen drop." The first student to get caught loses. For the teacher, the game is won when she or he is able to find a way to get the class to stop, already, with the pen dropping!

Bonus points are awarded students who can get the teacher to swear or convey threats. Bonus points are awarded to the teacher who gets a student to either confess to the act or rat out another student who is dropping a pen.

THE GAME OF "ONE UP" by *Christine Gargano*

The mind game of "One Up" is a board game with up to four pieces (two teacher pieces and two student pieces – you have to keep it fair!). The pieces are an apple and a ruler (that represent teachers) and a ribboned bow or a backwards cap (that represent students).

The board has a starting point and an ending point with spaces placed around a horseshoe, and players have to go through multiple rounds to fight to get to the end. Also, there are multiple sets of cards: the first deck of cards is the main deck; it is placed in the middle of the board and is used for each round. Main deck cards tell the scenario each player will face for each round. After the scenario card is flipped over, each player then picks one card from their own personal deck of cards (apple deck, ruler deck, ribboned bow deck, backwards cap deck).

After each player picks up a card from their personal deck, they have to evaluate the card to determine if their card is worthy of placing down as an appropriate response to the scenario at hand. If a student player and a teacher player both place down a card, they must pick again and determine if that card is worthy of beating the opponent's card. The player with the best rebuttal can advance a number of spaces (each card has its own number at its bottom). If you win using your first card, advance said number of spaces; if you win using two cards, add up the total number from both cards and advance that much.

Example of a Round
Main Deck Card: Teacher is teaching lesson to class. Student takes out a cell phone and starts texting during the lesson. Teacher catches student.

First Card from Student's Deck
For Student Player #1: Laugh at teacher (2 points).
For Student Player #2: Deny teacher accusation (and with 3 points, advance to next round, picking up another card).

First Card from Teacher's Deck
For Teacher Player #1: Threaten to call parent (and with 2 points, advance to next round, picking up another card).
For Teacher Player #2: Ignore student (1 point).

Player #2's Second Card from Student's Deck
Mock teacher (2 points).

Player #1's Second Card from Teacher's Deck
Kick student out of classroom (3 points).

Winner of Round: Teacher Player #1 for best rebuttal; teacher adds up the numbers on the bottom of each of Teacher's two cards (2 points plus 3 points for a total of 5 points) and moves 5 spaces on the horseshoe board toward its end.

And Round and Round it goes until eventually one Student or one Teacher wins the game.

A STORY ABOUT THE STORIED GAME CALLED "ANECDOTE" by *Daniel Garcia-Munoz Garcia*

Psychological games are often played by students and teachers; these games are difficult, but if you make sure to learn your opponent's weak points, you'll have a good chance to win.

Let me introduce you to my eighth-grade language teacher in Spain: she was a nice woman, probably in her thirties: she was old enough to have so many anecdotes that she would share with us but she was young enough to lack teaching experience. Or at least teenagers-teaching experience, for we all pretended to be interested in her stories and anecdotes just to waste time and miss our language lesson of the day.

Yes, we would do whatever it would take to mislead the teacher so that she would not achieve her goal – that was the objective of the game "Anecdote."

What about the rules? There were no rules; everything counted. As a warning, I would say that this mind game is not recommended for students who actually want to learn something (but there were no students like that among us).

This was work for a group: all of my classmates were allies with a common enemy to defeat. But was this really a mind game? Is it possible that one of the participants (the teacher) wasn't even aware that she was participating in a game? No, she was very aware of what was going on.

At first, we asked her many questions (how was your trip to Rome?, were you a good student when you were our age?, etc.) and just like that, she would start talking and talking, flattered that we had an interest in her.

However, after a while she realized she was being fooled. "No, guys, enough with the talk. Let's open our books. Page 15," she would say. We would run out of ideas, so the good girls in the class would ask her about her marriage life (something she loved discussing, especially with the girls).

"Not now, girls. I'm not going to fall for that!" Finally, when we were just about to open our books believing there was no hope for us, someone would come up with something like: "You know, Pedro, the math teacher, told us it is a fact that people who study science are more intelligent than people who study the humanities." She would get mad at that teacher's comment and give us a 40-minute speech about how people who study the humanities have usually more culture.

Check – and checkmate!

As all the **Staying After School** games you've just "played" demonstrate, game-playing among students and teachers is frequently a serio-comic combative affair with students serious about trying to delay any real learning on their part and teachers serious about trying to keep a challenging class on track and on task for the lesson that they carefully prepared and thoughtfully planned.

And, since most of us have been there in one role or another (including as game spectators), why don't you have some writing fun and recall, recreate, and play a classroom mind game of your own? And don't forget to give it a catchy name!

5

Up the Down Staircase, or, "Dear Sir or Madam, Let It Be a Challenge to You"

*U*P THE DOWN STAIRCASE, this chapter's featured school novel, is *the* end-of-term bookend for any course in school-set literature that begins with the novel *THE BLACKBOARD JUNGLE*. Published exactly a decade after Evan Hunter's conventionally structured and often fairly grim examination of a New York City high school in the early 1950's, Bel Kaufman's rather weirdly structured serio-comic 1964 New York City high school novel *UP THE DOWN STAIRCASE* is also in a class by itself.

Based on Kaufman's own three-and-half page magazine short story and composed by an author whose original language was Yiddish, *UP THE DOWN STAIRCASE* was written in strikingly colloquial English — and then went on, over the decades, to be translated into at least twenty other languages. But whatever the language in which it was being read, Kaufman's wish for the ten-page opening chapter of *UP THE DOWN STAIRCASE* was always the same: "Read it aloud, reader, read it aloud."

From the novel's eye-and-ear-catching opening words – "Hi, teach!" – Chapter 1 of *UP THE DOWN STAIRCASE* is hardly all noise and never nonsense; instead, it is a veritable and challenging cacophony of sounds interrupting other sounds. Here are that cacophony's first seventy lines:

Hi, teach!
Looka her? She's a teacher?
Who she?
Is this 304? Are you Mr. Barringer?
    No, I'm Miss Barrett.
I'm supposed to have Mr. Barringer.
    I'm Miss Barrett.
You the teacher? You so young.
Hey she's cute! Hey, teach, can I be in your class?
    Please don't block the doorway. Please come in.
Good afternoon, Miss Barnet.
    Miss Barrett. My name is on the blackboard. Good morning.
O, no! A dame for homeroom?
You want I should slug him, teach?
Is this homeroom period?
    Yes. Sit down, please.
I don't belong here.
We gonna have you all term? Are you a regular or a sub?
There's not enough chairs!
    Take any seat at all.
Hey, where do we sit?
Is this 309?
Someone swiped the pass. Can I have a pass?
What's your name?
    My name is on the board.
I can't read your writing.

I gotta go to the nurse. I'm dying.
Don't believe him, teach. He ain't dying!
Can I sharpen my pencil in the office?
Why don't you leave the teacher alone, you bums?
Can we sit on the radiator? That's what we did last term.
Hi, teach! You the homeroom?
Pipe down, you morons! Don't you see the teacher's
trying to say something?

Please sit down. I'd like to –
Hey, the bell just rung!
How come Mrs. Singer's not here? She was in this room
last term.
When do we go home?
The first day of school, he wants to go home already!

That bell is your signal to come to order. Will you please –
Can I have a pass to a drink of water?
You want me to alphabetize for you?
What room is this?

This is room 304. My name is on the board: Miss Barrett. I'll have you for homeroom all term, and I hope to meet some of you in my English classes. Now, someone once said that first impressions –
English! No wonder!
Who needs it?
You give homework?

First impressions, they say, are lasting. What do we base our first –
Yes? Do you belong in this class?
No. Mr. McHabe wants Ferone right away.

Who?
McHabe.

Whom does he want?
Joe Ferone.

Is Joe Ferone here?

Him? *That's a laugh!*
He'll show up when he feels like it.

Put down that window-pole, please. We all know that first impressions – Yes?
Is this 304?

Yes. You're late.
I'm not late. I'm absent.

You are?
I was absent all last term.

Well – sit down.
I can't. I'm dropping out. You're supposed go sign my
Book Clearance from last term.

Do you owe any books?
I'm not on the Blacklist! That's a yellow slip. This here
is a green!
Hey, isn't the pass back yet?
Quit your shoving!
He started it, teach!

I'd like you to come to order, please. I'm afraid we won't have time for the discussion on first impressions I had planned. I'm passing out –
Hey, she's passing out!
Give her air!

–Delaney cards. You are to fill them out at once while I take attendance from the Roll Book…

And this kind of thing (did you find it frustrating to read?) goes on for seven additional pages in this classic novel (perhaps *the* novel) about the American way of school life – and the "there's-no-place-like-homeroom" atmosphere gets more intrusively chaotic with the introduction of student aides bearing written notices from the administration that must immediately be read to all students who are expected, of course, to "listen carefully."

And, as a bonus, here is a bizarre but representative sampling of the public address system's announcements that soon start to come fast and furious:

- *Please ignore previous instructions in Circular #3, Paragraphs 5 and 6, and follow the following (special assembly schedule for the day);*
- *The school library is your library. All students are encouraged to use it at all times.… The library will be closed to students until further notice to enable teachers to use it as a workroom for their PRC (permanent record card) entries;*
- *To All Teachers: A Blue Pontiac parked in front of school has been overturned by some students. If the following license is yours…;*
- *Please disregard the bells. Students are to remain in their homerooms until the warning bell rings.*

But, of course, Miss Sylvia Barrett's homeroom students have already fled the room because, as one of them declares as he exits into the mobbed hallway, "When the bell rings, we're supposed to *go!*" Anyone think they're on their way to the library? Odds, anyone, that they're checking out the overturned blue Pontiac?

Staying After School student and what-if writer *Claudia Ng* explains her choice of metaphor for the opening ten pages of *UP THE DOWN STAIRCASE*:

> *A cacophony is reminiscent of a symphony orchestra playing music badly, just as there is no harmony in the opening scene in Bel Kaufman's classic school-set novel when newbie high school English teacher Miss Sylvia Barrett steps into her classroom for her first day of teaching. The teacher – the*

musical conductor in charge of setting everything in motion, everything in order – is confronted with challenges that prevent her from imparting knowledge, or even properly introducing herself to these high school students. The inadequacies of supplies, the rowdiness of the pupils, the administrative directives that continue to pile up on her desk all formulate together to become an untamable whirlwind. The classroom becomes an assault on the senses.

Miss Barrett is severely outnumbered by kids that have no wish to entertain her thoughts – or even listen. The novel provides snippets of conversation: when Miss Barrett says she is "passing out" (Delaney cards to be filled out with each student's information) she doesn't even get to finish her sentence before a kid tells everyone to give the teacher some air because she is "passing out." The multitude of distinct personalities present reveals the character of children in classroom settings all over the world, as they have not yet learned to subdue themselves for the greater good.

The opening scene in UP THE DOWN STAIRCASE is as dramatic as going to see a concert by an orchestra of second-rate musicians who have resisted rehearsals from their conductor. In going to school, you must adjust yourself to the mindset of learning – just as going to hear an orchestra play asks for respect that the music be listened to. A school is a special place in which the teacher is asked to perform, and everything must be adjusted – fine-tuned – so that the final performance is perfect.

Readers who honor author Kaufman's wish that at least the first few pages of Chapter 1 of *UP THE DOWN STAIRCASE* be read out loud (regardless of the language it has been published in) sense (as in "feel") the chapter's sense (as in "meaning"): they are immediately thrown into the hectic and frustrating experience for both teacher and student of continual interruption, jarring juxtapositions, and jagged junctures: the sound of urban school life.

As Sylvia Barrett attempts to introduce herself, take attendance, learn her students' names (and faces), establish order and sequence (and, it turns out, make a teaching point, if she can find a teaching moment – about the importance of "first impressions"), there is out-of-control cacophony and anything but order and harmony.

The sound of Miss Barrett's voice (not to mention, but let's: the meaning of her sentences) is repeatedly interrupted by students entering the room tardy, then late, then later; by student monitors with memos and circulars "for your immediate attention"; by students wanting to leave the room right now for a slew of reasons (never to return?); by annoyingly frequent public address announcements over the classroom's loudspeaker from administrators (we're talking about you, Assistant Principal McHabe) who believe they should command attention over and above any teaching and learning that might be going on (and then who get back on the p.a. system – "pardon the interruption!" – to countermand their previous commands).

And speaking, as Miss Barrett was trying to, of first impressions, what is a reader's first impression just a few pages into this novel of urban school life? High school for both its teachers and students is mainly meaningless confusion bordering on chaos (sound and sense signifying what?). If this classroom "jumble" constitutes teaching, can starting-out teacher Sylvia Barrett survive as a teacher? More critically, and forget burnout: can Miss Barrett survive *her first day* of teaching?

And speaking of the "jumble" of teaching, just a year after the national release of the film *BLACKBOARD JUNGLE* in 1955, an animated short inspired by it and its famous title on the "it-should-be-obvious-to everyone" secret behind successful teaching (by the famous

Hollywood cartooning team of Hanna and Barbera, and you can find it on YouTube) was in America's movie houses. Its title: "The Blackboard Jumble."

Welcome to the wild!

But what kind of non-wild welcome did newbie Sylvia Barrett of *UP THE DOWN STAIRCASE* receive from her academic high school's seasoned principal (the master, main, or "principal" teacher, Dr. Maxwell E. Clarke) before Calvin Coolidge High School's returning students got around to "hi, teaching" her to their school?

Staying After School student and what-if writer ***Jamal Stovall*** captures the almost smarmy egoism and bureaucratic "education-ese" and "bs" of Principal Clarke on that day after summer vacation that new and returning teachers arrived to start the new academic year:

> *(First musing to himself before speaking) This school would fall apart without me!*

> *(And then speaking aloud to the assembled faculty) It is with great pleasure that I welcome each of you amazing and remarkable teachers back to the unique and exclusive Calvin Coolidge High School. I am sure your summer was filled with you discovering innovative and creative ways to engage our gifted and talented students.*

> *I needn't remind you of our commitment to diligence, accuracy, and promptness, which are essential in carrying out all administrative instructions.*

As the new semester dawns, I am proud to be the principal, your principal, here at Calvin Coolidge High School. Take with you my perseverance and my strength, knowing that education is "e duco." For you teachers that are new, "e duco" means "leading out of." As educators you must help and encourage the students to unlock the potential and knowledge that is unbeknownst to them.

I look forward to talking to all of you teachers during my open door policy, which is currently closed for repair. Please feel free to leave me a note during this construction, and allow 2 to 8 business days for a response.

Not surprisingly, the cast of characters for *UP THE DOWN STAIRCASE* is a diverse portrait gallery of troubled and troubling adolescents who are, as Kaufman wrote in the introduction to a later edition of the novel, all in their own way crying out "Here I am! Care about me!" This collective portrait is made up of "the class comedian," "the sycophantic politician," "the over-ripe girl bursting with sexuality," "the black boy with a chip on his shoulder," "the Puerto Rican boy who finds himself," and "the silent girl who doesn't find herself."

Off to the side and frequently out of the frame is the angry dropout (but periodic drop-in) Joe Ferone, the student for whom Sylvia Barrett will most want to "make a difference." Will she succeed and save Joe from himself?

Staying After School students and what-if writers were free to become any one of these *UP THE DOWN STAIRCASE* students (regardless of gender). ***Evan Wezik*** chose to clone himself as "The Hawk," the anonymous student who only communicates with Miss Barrett through her inspired in-class suggestion box:

Suggestion Entry #1: Why is there always so much homework to do? Assignment after assignment! Way too much! Well, it doesn't matter. This is the last time I'm writing!

—The Hawk

Suggestion Entry #2: Maybe teach something more interesting or something. Or don't. It doesn't matter to me 'cause this is the last time I'm writing to you.

—The Hawk

Suggestion Entry #3: Don't be so hard on the students for being late or absent. There is a lot that goes on you don't know about. Okay, you won't hear from me again.

—The Hawk

Suggestion Entry #4: Why don't you tell that principal of ours to quit with all the memos and letters! It's very distracting. I would tell him, but this is the last time I'm writing so I don't really care.

—The Hawk

Suggestion Entry #5: Do you really have to leave this school? I was even considering writing more. But if you're leaving I guess it doesn't matter so this will be my last note.

—The Hawk

Suggestion Entry #6: I'm glad you decided to stay. I guess I'll write to you again soon.

—The Hawk

Fellow **Staying After School** student-writers, of course, became other Kaufman characters with their own idiosyncratic suggestion-box notes.

However, these "listen-to-me" notes were just one of the many different kinds of "pieces of paper" that Kaufman devised and used throughout her novel as the inspired building blocks of her uniquely structured narrative arc. (The "Dear Sir or Madam" salutation on letters to *named* recipients is – stranger than fiction! – absolutely real. And this writer still remembers being told to "let it be a challenge to you" by the head of school guidance at his first teaching job more than half a century ago.)

All of the following "pieces of paper" (and oral communications) appear in Kaufman's novel and were up for what-if wondering and creative extrapolation:

- items for placing in a classroom's suggestion box;
- administrators' memos and directives filed away in desk drawers or wastepaper baskets (pre-shredder days);
- items in the Calvin Coolidge High School newspaper;
- bulletin board displays on the walls of the school's corridors;
- schoolwide public address announcements;
- faculty conference minutes;
- a teacher's lesson plan;
- a student's minutes on a teacher's lesson;
- a chair's evaluative comments on a teacher's lesson;
- gossip in the faculty lounge;
- reports (to teachers) from school administrators;
- excerpts from letters or notes (between adult friends, between colleagues, between teachers and students);
- official letters from "The Board of Ed" in downtown Brooklyn.

These building blocks (which the inevitable Hollywood film version of the novel was unable to recreate or find cinematic equivalents of) so structure the novel that they can be found in all 58 of its chapters; here are just some of the chapter titles (with my interpretive comments in italics) of a school book that both credibly *and* incredibly captures the zeitgeist of urban education in the United States of America in the late 1950's and early 1960's:

- **Let It Be a Challenge To You**
  (*to the teacher, that is – because nobody else has a clue what to do about "it"!*)

- **From Miss Barrett's Letterbox**
  (*in the main or general office, but rarely in correct alphabetical order and always too high up to be reached*)

- **From Miss Barrett's Wastebasket**
  (*"From a Teacher's Wastebasket" was the magazine title of Kaufman's original three-and-a-half-page short story that UP THE DOWN STAIRCASE got expanded from*)

- **From the Suggestion Box**
  (*The Hawk and others*)

- **Over the Time-Clock**
  (*like factory workers, teachers inserted punch cards into clock-like machines to record their exact times of arrival and departure; "important" notices posted over the time-clock could rarely be read because of the line of teachers waiting behind you to punch in or out*)

- **Please Do Not Erase**
  (*guess what always happens to those words!*)

- **Neatly, In Ink**
  (*you should have brought a spare; and, no, for some reason but no explanation why, pencil just won't do*)

- **Unfortunate Incident**
  (*putting it mildly?*)

- **I'm Not Cheating, I'm Left-Handed**
  (*right!*)

- **It Has Come to My Attention**
  (*uh, oh!*)

- **What Did I Miss?**
  (*when I cut class or was absent, if I may ask*)

- **"Teacher for a Day" Day**
  (*putting the "clone" in cyclone*)

- **A for Effort**
  (*not an "E"?*)

- **Dear Sir or Madam**
  (*whose actual full name is right there just above these words*)

- **Hi, Pupe!**
  (*the now famous closing line of the novel; Kaufman planned it from the start of her writing of the novel version of UP THE DOWN STAIRCASE to be a meaningful bookend to the casual "Hi, Teach!" that opens the book*)

Here is a short "building block" request from a teacher at Calvin Coolidge High School addressed to the school custodian as a what-if piece of writing by **_Jamal Stovall_**:

> _To Custodian:_
>
> _Please be advised that one of our more adventurous and amazing students tested the strength of our classroom windows in an awe-inspiring experiment and the remains need to be cleared up as soon as possible._

Let it be a challenge to you!

6

Correspondences: To the Misses Barrett, Brodie, and Honey – and With Love to the Two Sirs

A ll **Staying After School** students and what-if writers were asked as part of their course work to create imaginative "correspondences" (literally as posted letters and figuratively as pedagogical similarities) between teacher Sylvia Barrett of *UP THE DOWN STAIRCASE* and "a colleague" from another fictional work studied in "The Teacher and Student in Literature" course (in which all characters had to be true to themselves and to their "home" work of literature).

What-if writer ***Georgette Kadianakis*** decided to have Sylvia Barrett attend a teaching seminar being offered by cult-of-personality teacher Jean Brodie of the 1961 Muriel Spark novel *THE PRIME OF MISS JEAN BRODIE* (and 1969 film of the same name). After the seminar, Miss Barrett gets some one-on-one time with the famous (infamous?) Scottish teacher from Edinburgh's exclusive Marcia Blaine School for Girls. Miss Brodie is in her "prime" as a woman and teacher and is lecturing on "How to Influence Your Students." Miss Barrett's "prime" concern is to get some expert advice on how to handle and help her most difficult student, Joe Ferone. Here are some excerpts from their conversation:

Miss Barrett: I understand from your seminar that being in your prime is the reason why you are able to greatly influence your Brodie set of girls. This is my first year of teaching and I'm not sure if I'm in my prime, but I also want to influence my students as much as I can. Am I failing before I start?

Miss Brodie: Not necessarily, but confidence in yourself is definitely key to influencing your students to be the crème de la crème. If you yourself are not the crème de la crème, how will your students be? You need to be in your prime in order to fully achieve your goal. Start by fixing any uncertainties in your life.

Miss Barrett: Very interesting. I did start trying to influence one of my students this year, Joe Ferone, and he is resisting me very much. Joe is very smart and has potential but he has the habit of dropping in and dropping out. I believe that I should listen to the voices of my students and their parents. Any suggestions for what I can do even if I'm not in my prime yet?

Miss Brodie: I suggest that you and this Joe Ferone try to reach your primes together. Find out his interests and how they connect to your own. Spark any possible interests in the classical arts – there is so much to appreciate. Figure out your dream for him and try to make that his reality. If you're successful with Joe Ferone, then maybe that will be how you reach your prime.

What-if writer *Gabriela Carela* chose to create a sent-through-the-post correspondence between the American Sylvia Barrett (of the somewhat autobiographical 1964 Kaufman novel) and British teacher Mark Thackery (of the 1967 semi-autobiographical film *TO SIR, WITH LOVE*). In the movie, Mark Thackery is largely the fictional stand-in for E. R. Braithwaite ("Sir"), the author of the 1959 novel-memoir with the same title as the film.

In the book, Thackery is actually called by the author's last name, Braithwaite. Whatever his name, he's a well-educated black man with the *calling* to be an engineer and the advanced degree in engineering to go with it.

However, Thackery/Braithwaite has been repeatedly racially discriminated against in his chosen career field. In order to have any kind of professional job and make some kind of living, Braithwaite/Thackery finds he must accept a rather undesirable teaching position that has only become available to him in a South London lower-class ghetto high school (much, but not exactly, like Rick Dadier's *BLACKBOARD JUNGLE* vocational high school in New York City) because the regularly appointed teacher can no longer take the disrespectful attitudes of his "delinquent" students and suddenly quits.

In her creative extensions of all three of these works of school-based literature – *UP THE DOWN STAIRCASE* and the book and film versions of *TO SIR, WITH LOVE* – what-if writer *Gabriela Carela* chose to cast Barrett and Thackery/Braithwaite as originally fellow undergraduate college students who became close friends before their lives went off in different directions after graduation.

October 8
Dear Thackery,

The beginning of this school year has been more than I could ever have imagined or planned for. I am in charge of a group of students – but are they really students? I am so swamped by circulars that I haven't actually taught any English!

Best,
Barrett

October 22
Dear Barrett,

You are certainly not alone. I am desperate to find work in the engineering field. Although I can see the potential these kids have, they have no desire to learn! I have attempted to teach them day after day, trying not to lose my patience because, believe me, they have tried it all! They want me to lose it!

Sincerely,
Thackery

November 10

Oh my dear friend, I have almost lost it one too many times, but my biggest problem is not the children! It's the adults I'm dealing with, who seem to be most concerned with punishing children instead of rewarding them when deserved. The "administrator" is so preoccupied with "maintaining order," he forgets it is children he is leading, not prisoners. I am fed up with the system, Thackery, reading through assignments I see grown kids still struggling to read and write correctly. I don't blame them. I blame the system that has reinforced their weaknesses and stepped on their strengths. I am sorry to sound so negative, Thackery, but I am so horrified. I've considered taking a college professor's position that has been offered for the next term. What do you think?

Best,
Barrett

November 28

Barrett, you are a born teacher! It has always been your lifelong goal to teach and make a difference in the lives of children. I, too, am very frustrated with the societal system, most of all, but I can understand how difficult it is for you to want to teach and be constantly reprimanded and interrupted. Even though my issues with kids are a bit different, I, although not a born teacher, can appreciate that all that these kids need is guidance and a strong hand that tells them things about how it is. I have faith that you can also tell this "administrator" you speak of exactly how it is you intend to run your classroom! After all, it is your classroom and even the highest authority must respect that.

In regard to moving to a different school to teach older groups, I think you should do what you feel is right to you. However, I don't think you will feel right leaving your current kids half way through a school year knowing you have made some difference in their outlooks of education and English, your subject! You are a great teacher and based on what you have told me about this group of kids in the past, you can make these children find a new appreciation of education and hope that they can get more than they think out of life!

You can do this,
Thackery

December 24

Thackery, my dear friend, happy holidays! I have been very busy (of course mostly with circulars and pointless dead-end meetings) but I have great news: even though I am so incredibly displeased with the way things are run around here, I have decided to take up your advice. I had something like an enlightening experience occur to me. I hurt my foot in a school-organized play while I attempted to help back stage (horrible, I know). As I was sitting in a hospital bed writing letters to my friend Ellen (remember her?) and to you, I received some letters from my students, and I am surprised at what some of them had to say. They want me to come back! I can't explain the feeling I have within me but I am eager to be on my feet and in my classroom! I am wishing you the happiest of holidays and I hope you, too, are feeling more comfortable at your school (even if it's not what you wanted professionally).

Best,
Barrett

January 5
My dear Barrett,

I am so excited to hear from you! Happy holidays! I am so sorry to hear about your foot, yet so happy that it has made you

*realize how much potential you truly have! As for me, I scored
an engineering position for next year, and I am happy as can be,
because I was able to attain the opportunity. However, believe it
or not, I am second-guessing it all. I don't know anymore. My
kids have taught me so much and the class behind them has
shown clear indications of needing guidance; if I leave, I will
miss out on the shot of perhaps guiding these astray children.
I am conflicted, and, yet, the answers to my own questions
seem so clear. Barrett, I am glad that you are okay and I look
forward to hearing all about your new approach.*

The very best,
Thackery

An aside: in an interesting piece of movie casting, the black
American actor Sidney Poitier appears in both the film version of *THE
BLACKBOARD JUNGLE* (1955) and the film version of *TO SIR, WITH
LOVE* (1967). In the former he plays the troublesome African-American
high school student Gregory Miller; in the latter, he plays the troubled
teacher Mark Thackery.

Some of the teaching and learning similarities between *TO SIR, WITH
LOVE, THE BLACKBOARD JUNGLE,* and *UP THE DOWN STAIRCASE* can
be seen in the following playlet by **Staying After School** student and what-if
writer ***Christen Schuchardt.***

Set in a coffee shop in New York City during the summer following
Sylvia Barrett's first year of teaching, Barrett and Rick Dadier (now a
veteran high school English teacher) have been brought together by their
respective school administrators and supervisors, Assistant Principal
McHabe and English Chair Stanley):

Dadier: So tell me, then, tell me how this year was for you. After all, my longtime English chair, Mr. Stanley, mentioned to me that you and I may have had some similar experiences.

Barrett: You actually remember your first year? After all those crazy years of North Manual Trades Vocational, you can still differentiate your first year from the rest?

Dadier (lightly chuckling): Of course I can! And believe me, you, too, will always be able to remember yours. Would you like to hear about my first year before you enlighten me with your story?

Barrett: Please!

Dadier: Well, as you may or may not know, my first year was not easy. And neither was yours – I know that much, but while my first year was tough, I learned something, something important. You see, there was this one student, Gregory Miller, I was determined to reach out to him. I didn't want him going down the wrong path. Just because he was in a vocational high school, I didn't want him to feel like he had no opportunities in life (pause); did you have a student like that too?

Barrett: Why, yes; yes I did! His name was Joe Ferone (pause) but I was unsuccessful in getting through to him (pause). But you, did you get through to Gregory?

Dadier: Yes, in a sense, I did. But in doing so I also seemed to have made an impact on my other students' careers as well; maybe not as great an impact, but it was more than they first had.

*Barrett: Why (shocked) it seems as though Mr. McHabe and
Mr. Stanley were right to introduce me to you, for I too had
a similar experience. You see, I did not successfully reach out
to Joe Ferone, but I realized that I had reached out to all my
other students. I didn't realize it until I nearly left; I didn't leave,
though, just so you know. See, it was that realization that made
me stay. I may not have impacted Joe's life in the way I intended
but just knowing that my students cared for me, wanted me back
after my unfortunate accident that put me in the hospital, it
was enough to make me stay (pause, just in thought); I'm glad
I stayed, I'm glad I made some difference in their lives.*

*Dadier: Well, I'm glad you stayed, too; it seems to have made
an equally great difference on you.*

Barrett: It has!

*Dadier: You know, you and I are rather similar in more ways than
it would seem. I had moments in my first year where I wanted to
quit; I've even had moments more recently where I wanted to quit!
Teaching is not easy. Teaching English is not easy!*

Barrett: I am aware!

*Dadier: But trust me, if you still have moments of hesitation,
remember that moment in your first year that inspired you
to keep going. That's why I still remember my first year at
North Manual Trades: for every now and then I need to reflect
and remember those students – my first students and how
important a teacher can be in the life of a student. So you will
remember this first year and those students, especially when
you think quitting is better than teaching.*

Barrett: All right, you have a point, one which I'll never forget (pause). Well, before I depart, Mr. Dadier, I'd like to leave you with an interesting statistic.

Dadier: Okay then; let me hear it.

Barrett: Did you know that there are more school children in New York City than there are soldiers in the U. S. Army?

Dadier (chuckling): Well, then it sounds like we may need to continue teaching for quite a while!

Curtain.

Finally in these imaginative what-if trips up the down staircase, Sylvia Barrett gets to meet two characters from British author Roald Dahl's 1988 young adult novel *MATILDA*: precocious pupil Matilda and her sweet teacher, Miss Honey. The monstrous headmistress Miss Trunchbull – "My idea of a perfect school is one that has no children in it at all" – has been banished from this casual conversation by its **Staying After School** student and what-if writer ***Messay Kassi***:

(Mid-way through a conversation about school between Matilda and Sylvia Barrett and set in New York City)

Matilda: I love school. School is better than being at home, and the only thing that is better than being at school is being in the library.

Barrett: Wow, I wish all of my students in the classroom were like you!

Matilda: And I wish that my headmistress, Miss Trunchbull, was like you. She was so mean to me and I was only five years old! If it wasn't for Miss Honey, I don't know if I would've made it.

Barrett: So, what was Miss Honey like?

Matilda: She was extremely nice and extremely caring. She always made sure that I was learning since I was always ahead of the other students in the class; she paid close attention to me. Miss Honey takes pride in her teaching and we need more teachers to be that way.

Barrett: Hmmm. I would love to meet Miss Honey. I'm sure that we could relate in many ways, even outside the classroom. She sees you like how I see my students. You seem to be a student with high intelligence and involvement, and I wish all students could be just as engaged in their learning. Only if there were a way.

(Miss Honey enters the room)

Matilda: This is her. Miss Barrett, Miss Honey. We were just talking about you, Miss Honey.

Miss Honey: What a pleasure to meet you, Miss Barrett. Are you a teacher as well?

Barrett: You can call me Sylvia. Yes, I teach English at Calvin Coolidge High School. I'm actually going to be Matilda's teacher in the fall.

Miss Honey: What a lucky teacher you must be! Matilda is a great student and terrific young lady. It's been so many years, I could only imagine how much more grown she is now.

Barrett: Yes, yes she is! She came into my classroom as an eighth-grader during an open house and saw me teaching. She saw how chaotic the classroom environment was and waited until the class was over to tell me that she will be attending this high school just because she loved the way I taught and how I reminded her of you.

Miss Honey: Oh, wow, what a fantastic way to meet Matilda. I wish I could have a hundred Matildas, but also having less motivated and ambitious students is what makes this profession so unique and worthwhile. It creates trial-and-error situations in which you find out what style of teaching and learning works for the class as a whole or for specific students.

Barrett: That is very true, I couldn't agree more! This is something I have been trying to find when I teach. My students always interrupt each other and essentially can't properly communicate with one another, and they should be able to, especially at this age. I try to teach them by showing them through my own actions and by correcting them and portraying a very patient attitude.

Miss Honey: And I think that's a great start. It shows you care for the teaching profession. I think a lot has to do with self-motivation and establishing the importance of school with the home. Matilda is a unique example, but she is also self-motivated and naturally into books and learning – possibly having Matilda in your classroom will cause other students to look at her as a model as to how to function properly in a classroom and realize the importance of education.

Barrett: I certainly hope so. She is a wonderful person and maybe the interaction of students and developing a relationship with students outside the classroom will help a student to make the decision to listen and pay attention in class the way that they should. Maybe developing after-school programs that don't involve school work, just once a week where we talk to students, in groups or individually, and just talk about anything. This can lead to changes in the classroom and personal development that will help our students in multiple ways.

Miss Honey: That is absolutely genius! I love the idea and the scheduling. I would love to be a part of that and maybe we can help each other out. I can come to your school once a week and partake in that weekly activity and vice-versa. We can even create fun educational games that the students will enjoy and maybe even bring in a guest speaker to connect with their interests.

Barrett: I love it! I love it! Let's continue to communicate about this in the near future. It's getting late and the last bus leaves within five minutes.

Miss Honey: Great! Keep in touch!

Curtain.

7

Instructions on How to Belch on Command – and Other Teaching Moments

I don't remember and can't locate where I came upon the following maxim about teaching and learning, but here it is for what it's worth (and that, in my opinion, is a lot):

Teach me, I forget; show me, I remember; involve me, I understand.

I do remember where I saw this maxim most originally illustrated in a work of literature: it was a scene late in E. L. Konisburg's 1996 young adult novel *THE VIEW FROM SATURDAY* that featured Mrs. Olinski and two students in her class of sixth graders.

In a kind of mind board game involving Team Teacher Olinski and Team Student Knapp-and-Ham (with the rest of the pupils as avid spectators and potential supporting players), Mrs. Olinski, before the

opening move of the game, is seated at her desk, sorting out papers to
be returned to her pupils. As E. L. Konisgsburg tells it:

*The room was quiet until a student in the back of the room let
out an enormous belch and said, not too sincerely, "Sorry."*

*Mrs. Olinski continued sorting papers before looking up.
"Hamilton Knapp?"*

"Yes, ma'am," he answered.

"Would you please come to the front?"

*He walked slowly, watching her, a half smile on his face.
She let him take his time. Before he reached the front of
the classroom, someone launched another belch. Its sound
rocketed forward, and the laughter that followed traveled
the same trajectory. Mrs. Olinski waited until Ham reached
the front of the room before asking, "Jared Lord, would you
please join Mr. Knapp?"*

*Jared also took his time, and Mrs. Olinski did not rush him
either. As he ambled down his row toward the front of the
room, smiling faces lifted and tilted toward him like the
broad front faces of sunflowers as they follow the sun across
heaven. Mrs. Olinski allowed that, too.*

*"Now, Mr. Knapp and Mr. Lord," she said, "I would like the
two of you to teach the entire class how to belch on command.
Please describe the process for all of us." She picked up a
piece of chalk from the ledge. "Which one of you wants to
take notes on the instructions we are about to receive?"*

Neither volunteered, so she thrust the chalk into Knapp's hand. "I think you enjoy writing on the blackboard, Mr. Knapp," she said. Ham took the chalk. The class registered its approval with body language that was the equivalent of silent applause.

The class waited. "I'll help you with the spelling," Mrs. Olinski said.

Ham began to clown around, rolling his eyes and saying, "Well, first you …."

The rest of the kids tightened their stomachs, opened their mouths, and tried to figure out how to explain a belch. Jared stood at the blackboard – empty-handed, awkward, uncomfortable – and he too, tried to figure it out. Knapp made another attempt. "Well, first you …."

Mrs. Olinski allowed them to stand there until three minutes seemed like thirty. Then she sent them back to their seats. "Since you cannot describe what you have done, I would call belching loudly to interrupt our class an unspeakable act. Unspeakable. And because you cannot explain how to do it, I would say that you cannot teach it either." She paused, locked eyes first with Knapp and then with Lord before adding, "But I can. If I choose to, I can explain how to belch on command, and I could teach you. If I choose."

She looked at Knapp and Lord again, her nostrils flared slightly, and then slowly turned her head to the class and added, "But I don't. The front of the classroom is privileged territory. There are only two reasons for you to be there. One,

you are teaching something to the rest of the class or, two,
you have been invited. From now on, the only tricks that I
am willing to put up with are those that you can first explain
and then teach."

Staying After School and what-if writers were invited, *eventually*, to come to the "privileged territory" of the front of the classroom to describe, explain, and teach the entire class "something" or "some thing" (they are not synonymous!): a behavior, activity, or skill that the play-at-teacher individual had practiced with a writing partner and now was strongly motivated to teach others. Over time and in every one of the partnerships, each individual's "how to" lesson plan was repeatedly revised based on "learner" feedback. Or as Geoffrey Chaucer more succinctly and poetically put it in *THE CANTERBURY TALES*, each pair came to "gladly learn" and "gladly teach."

Of course, any "instructional objective" was allowed – just as long as it would not embarrass teacher, student, or class. The creative results follow on these next pages – except for one of the very best "how to" lessons produced that, although it was not deemed "unspeakable" by the writer, the paired learner, or me, would definitely be considered "unprintable" by the publisher of this book. (Sorry, no "director's cut" or "bonus feature" is available.)

One of the more interesting realizations that came out of this teaching/learning project was that if there was something that you really liked knowing how to do and, modestly, thought yourself really quite good at, you were soon surprised to discover that you really didn't exactly understand how you knew what you knew. In order to teach "something or some thing" to someone else, you almost always had to figure out (learn!) how to consciously and deliberately teach it to yourself. Many expert teachers have discovered this truth early in their careers.

Staying After School student and what-if writer
Krenare Celaj explains "How to Master the Art of Waitressing":

> *Waitressing may look simple; however, there is a lot that goes into it. You have to deal with all different types of people and pleasing them is the key. After all, that is how you make your money.*
>
> *Patience: it sounds very clichéd, but having patience is critical. Many people are indifferent about what they want to order, and the more patient you are, the more they will appreciate you.*
>
> *Knowing the menu: Obvious? Not really. If someone asks for a certain dish, you need to describe it so well that it is clear that you know what you are talking about. People have food allergies, so you should know what it is that you are actually giving them. It also looks very good when you recommend a dish and the customer gets it and loves it.*
>
> *Smiling: a smile, especially when you've got a group of people, can go a long way. Compliment, smile, especially if they have kids, and try to interact with them. Some kids will persuade parents to tip you better.*
>
> *Speed and accuracy: you can't do anything about how long someone's food takes to be prepared; however, you should still linger by their table to remind them that you are around and on top of things. Accuracy is important; sometimes the kitchen is very busy or overwhelmed, so let's say a table asks for a salad with no onions: pick the onions off yourself with*

a utensil rather than bothering the kitchen about something small.

Appearance: make sure you look your best, and if you are a female, make sure your make-up is done. Generally speaking, the better you look, the more likely you are to get a better tip.

No distractions: getting distracted will be your biggest downfall if you are busy. Focus. Worry about your tables before anything else.

Being a helping hand: lend a helping hand to your co-workers because when you are overwhelmed you could use the help. Run their food and drink orders, even though it's their responsibility. You need the good karma.

Empathy: be empathetic with a customer; if they don't like something, try to fulfill their needs. However, don't be a pushover: try to be stern but not rude – some people like to take advantage.

Stories: if you're a student or a single parent, customers will love you. They'll ask you what you are studying and tell you how amazing it is that you work and go to college – and, most likely, give you a good tip.

Positivity: I mean it! It will allow you to stay in a good mood all day.

Staying After School student and what-if writer
Rachel Steinman narrates "How to Master the Art of Reading Aloud a Book to a Group of Little Children":

> *Before you can even start your story time you need to pick a good book to read. Look over a book for rhyming, songs, parts to skip, and parts to get kids to interact with the story. Then start your story time; generally you will attract your kids by announcing that it is about to begin in a loud excited voice.*
>
> *As you call children over, already be in the place where you will sit and read the book, otherwise a child might sit in your spot or behind your spot where they can't see the book. After most of the children are settled, introduce yourself and say hello to everyone. Introduce your book by title and begin. Hold the book completely open unless there are surprises on the opposite page. Never turn the book away from children and towards yourself. Hold the book to the side and instead turn your head around to read.*
>
> *If there is a large crowd, move the book, facing the children around the front of your body so that everyone can see. Depending on the length of your book, you want to stop every couple of pages to either have the children guess what happens next or act out something that has just happened in the story.*
>
> *Remember to project your voice to the back of the crowd and use voices if applicable and you are able. Continue on through to the end of the book. Thank everyone for reading with you or helping you out. You can sing a song that connects to the*

*book if you feel it's appropriate. End, finally, by thanking
everyone for coming and asking the children for high-fives.
Children love high-fives!*

Staying After School student and what-if writer
Jack Link visualizes "How to Have a Firm Handshake of Intimacy":

*First, make sure your right hand is free and without
condensation (regardless of how nervous you are).*

*Second, always rise if you're sitting, and consider your body
posture and the position of your head in relation to your
colleague.*

*Third, make sure when you're rising that you are focusing in
that moment, especially since it's very brief (and it's a first
impression).*

*Fourth, it's imperative to have eye contact on exchange of
greeting and a brief warm smile to accompany the pleasure
of meeting someone.*

*Fifth, when you're reaching out, keep your hand perpendicular,
neither palm down or up (dominant/submissive); open wide
and ensure optimal web/thumb contact. Try to wrap your
fingers around your partner's hand, as if giving a hug!*

*Sixth, once contact is made, lock your thumb and give a
firm grip – about as much as your partner. Shake from the
elbow – not the wrist! Release after a few pumps.*

Staying After School student and what-if writer
Raquel Levy instructs on "How to Binge-Watch an Entire Season in One Day":

> *Despite popular belief, aka my mother's, it is totally possible to binge an entire season of your favorite show in one day! However, full disclosure, there is a lot of self-loathing involved due to feelings of hitting peak laziness. Despite that minor setback, it is achievable, and here's how you do it either at the peak of the show's series, once you're already hooked, or after the first season of the series so you can power through those slower-paced episodes.*

> *It's all about preparation, so make sure you are well rested for the day to come. Set an alarm for about nine o'clock in the morning. If you are a teen, you might find this way too early, especially on the weekend; however, the early alarm is necessary so that you have more time to watch more episodes. Once you are awake, don't lie around in bed scrolling through various social media platforms because you will have time for this once you start binge watching the season.*

> *Right after this go to the kitchen and make sure to load up on snacks, coffee or tea, and water. Caffeine is essential to this method. Next, proceed to your desired viewing area. I like to switch off between my bed and my couch in the den. I recommend having two viewing areas to alternate between when you eventually get antsy. Like I said, this method is all about preparation.*

By this point you should have your snacks, streaming devices, and your viewing areas all prepped and ready. Now it is time to watch. I would advise closing all of your shades so you won't be able to see the day you're about to waste by staying in bed and watching TV. So, once you're ready, go ahead and press play! After watching one to two episodes you should note the length of the show's recap and theme song so you'll be able to skip over these segments and save precious seconds that, believe me, stack up.

If nature calls whilst binge-watching, either you can leave the show running or switch to the app on the phone that you have already downloaded in preparation for this moment. The app is highly recommended; this way you can stream when in the bathroom or even as you're moving from one viewing area to the next!

Make sure when you finish an episode to press "next episode" rather than waiting the fifteen seconds for the episode to change on its own. This is important for two reasons: the site will detect activity and not ask if you are "still watching" and it saves time so you can squeeze in more episodes. Depending on the length of the episodes and the season itself, you might need to stay up all hours of the night, so be prepared to sacrifice your beauty sleep for the sake of the season. You can stay awake by making sure you are caffeinated and by moving around so that you don't doze off. If all else fails, just leave the show playing and just listen to the voices (but, disclaimer, when I do this I tend to fall asleep!).

Staying After School student and what-if writer
Christine Gargano Enumerates the "Ten Ways to Be an Exceptional Friend":

I've had a successful best friendship with a fellow student in "The Teacher and Student in Literature" course for almost ten years. (No coincidence that we are in the course together!) How has our friendship been so successful? How did we continue to stay a tight unit throughout all those years while both of us were maturing and entering adulthood? Here are some tips on being a best friend:

1. Find common interests and don't be afraid to approach the other person first. As you know, Krenare (my longtime best friend Krenare Celaj), you and I originally did not get along. However, overcoming my fear of rejection from you, I approached you about something we may have shared in common and although we did not agree on the subject I presented, my tactic worked! I followed up by asking that we spend our lunch break together, and it just flowed from there. Never let fear hold you back.

2. With that being said, never be afraid to be true to yourself. You are who you are – and your best friend will always accept that. You may have different personality types but you should never change for the other person. Being fake will cause you to lose a best friend (as we have experienced many times throughout our friendships with other people). It is hard to pretend to be someone you are not, so always be true to who you are.

3. Don't hold things in. If you feel uncomfortable or have hard feelings toward your best friend, talk about it; it will hurt a friendship when you hold your feelings in. There will be times when speaking about how you feel about a situation or each other may be scary or hurtful, but not being truthful may leave you feeling resentment towards your best friend and maybe even cause you both to drift apart. Never keep your feelings in or hold secrets inside.

4. Speaking of secrets, a true key to friendship is trust. At times it may seem hard – or nearly impossible – to keep your best friend happy. To be a best friend does not take much: you just have to make sure you can trust one another about the really important aspects of your lives. Never tell someone a secret a friend wanted you to keep. A secret is a secret. What makes our friendship so successful is that it's almost like we are in a bubble. We can confide in each other about anything with one hundred percent confidence that our words will be respected and kept within our bubble.

5. Keep your word. If you say you're going to do something, do it. You know what they say: talk is cheap. Always follow through with what you say you are going to do. Best friends never doubt each other.

6. This is big: be loyal. Oh, loyalty: such a mystical concept of late. Through ups, and downs, and disagreements, always try to be attentive; work it out and be there for one another. Don't gossip about your best friend. Being part of a friendship is being proud of your friend: you should never bash your best friend or tear them down.

7. Spend time together. As we have gotten older and our work schedules and school journeys have changed, we have always found a way to make time to spend together. It may be necessary to sacrifice some of your time but sacrifice is not always bad: it is necessary to maintain a positive relationship.

8. Get to know your best friend's family. Our families are really important to us, even if they can sometimes be annoying, intrusive, and pesky. Getting to know your best friend's family shows them that you appreciate where they come from and are interested in knowing the people who are valuable in their life. As I don't really have any family besides my parents, getting to know your family allowed me to feel like I have a second home, a place to belong. It also brought us closer together in the process.

9. Avoid expectations. If you assume you know what your best friend's roles are, you could get disappointed and frustrated. Best friends are the most valuable friends you have, but they can't help or support you in every aspect of your life. Do not expect them to agree with everything or always say the things you want to hear. If you set expectations for your best friend that are too high, it will only leave you disappointed and defeated. Remember that no one is perfect – not even your best friend. Everyone has their own faults, and they need to work through them. Don't be mean to your best friend about their faults but help them work though them while asking for help on your own faults. Understand that your friend has feelings and it is best to focus on the faults that are the biggest threat to your friendship. Know what faults to ignore or let go of. Embrace one another's flaws while trying to help each other grow as a person.

10. Always be there! This is crucial. We have been through some very hard times together – times I wish never existed. It is so painful to see your best friend in pain or struggling through something difficult. At times, you may feel incredibly helpless and upset because you don't know how to make their pain go away. But although you may not be able to rid them of their pain, your presence in their life through these obstacles means more to the other person than you may expect. Being a best friend means being there for someone else for all the successful and painful stages of their life.

These rules may seem lengthy and over-detailed, but, trust me, being a best friend is not a difficult task at all. Friendship should never be hard. Krenare, being your best friend has been both enjoyable and rewarding – and I will always be proud. Shouldn't we be proud of something we have worked on?

8

The Only Thing That Distinguishes Teacher's Pest From Teacher's Pet Is a Single "S" That Stands for Special (Or Maybe Star-Student)

The author Leo Rosten once defined "humor" as "the affectionate communication of insight" and "the subtlest and chanciest of literary forms." Rosten's nine-star novel *THE EDUCATION OF H*Y*M*A*N K*A*P*L*A*N* (under the penname Leonard Q. Ross) has been called by literary critics not only a "hilarious, timeless tale" but also *the* classic tribute to the urban immigrant experience in and with American education. The title of Rosten's 1937 novel suggests an emphasis on "the Student" more than "the Teacher" since it begins with the words "the education of."

But think about it: you can't have one without the other – and most readers of this short novel would agree that Mr. Kaplan's night school adult ed teacher – the conventional and pedantic but concerned and frustrated Mr. Parkhill at the American Night Preparatory School for Adults – definitely learns a thing or two about teaching and learning from his "problem case," "star" student, and, arguably, "teacher's pet": the one-of-a-kind Mr. Kaplan. A challenging student to say the most!

Rosten fondly looks back on Pedagogue Parkhill in a 1959 sequel entitled *THE RETURN OF H*Y*M*A*N K*A*P*L*A*N*, writing in that novel's preface that as a teacher Mr. Parkhill had "infinite patience, kindliness, restraint, an incorruptible faith in man, and unshatterable faith in his perfectibility.... He seems to think that every man and woman on earth can be taught, can learn, can improve." He also "took a larger view of his responsibilities: to Mr. Parkhill the school was an incubator of Citizens. To imbue men and women of a dozen nations with the meaning of America – its past, its traditions, its aspirations – this, to Mr. Parkhill, was the greater work to which he had dedicated himself."

Set in immigrant-intense New York City during the worldwide Great Depression of the 1930's (not in Chicago where Rosten had briefly been an unaccredited substitute night school instructor), the first novel, *THE EDUCATION OF HYMAN KAPLAN*, consists of fifteen linked "character" studies, many of which had been previously published in magazines (and with the last of them the most memorable). These fifteen stories ("all true, but they never happened," Rosten later wrote) are all about students who are wrestling with a slippery English language syntax that must have been invented by a Torquemada-type torturer.

Something else quite special about this literary work on "the teacher and student" relationship is that not just a few but *all* of its narrative scenes take place in a classroom. Looking back on his writing of *THE EDUCATION OF HYMAN KAPLAN*, author Leo Rosten talks about the "strait-jacket" of a setting he was contemplating:

> *The locale could scarcely be less inspiring: a classroom, a*
> *classroom of a beginners' grade, a classroom of a beginners'*
> *grade in a night school, a classroom of a beginners' grade in*
> *a night school for adults, a classroom of a beginners' grade*
> *in a night school for adults presided over not by a rich, juicy*

*character, such as Samuel Johnson or Scaramouche, but a
terribly staid teacher named Parkhill.*

You may have noticed that I have left out Mr. Kaplan's stars in my
most recent references to the book's title (*he* would have noticed!). My
attribution policy is to do the stars for the title only on the very first
mention, even though Hyman Kaplan *always* "stars" his own name but
never anyone else's (spoiler alert: except *once* in a special tribute to his
teacher Mr. Parkhill).

While the young adult novel considered in Chapter 7 – *THE VIEW
FROM SATURDAY* – features mainly native-born elementary school
pupils working on their language acquisition skills in a 9:00 to 3:00
classroom, *THE EDUCATION OF HYMAN KAPLAN* features some
thirty-odd (and not-so-young-anymore) adult learners from a variety of
lands and cultures making up the salad bowl, if not the melting pot, of
the United States of America.

It turns out that many of these adult-school immigrants are male and
female Jews from Eastern Europe who are working hard to learn English
as their second language (a few other ethnic and religious immigrant
groups are represented as well). The Jews in Mr. Parkhill's class mostly
speak Yiddish, which is linguistically close to German, or they speak
English with a heavy Yiddish pronunciation (and intonation pattern and
accent), and they misspell it in writing in ways that are magnificent. Mr.
Kaplan, however, is in a linguistic and logical class by himself having
once recited, for example, the principal parts of "to eat" as "eat, ate,
full" and on another occasion given the opposite of "inhale" as "dead."

Nevertheless, he and all the other immigrant students share a
common goal: to pass the naturalization test to become American
citizens – that's their "American dream" (one still very much in the news
these days in a country that is historically "a nation of immigrants").
The official name of the class says it all: "English–Americanization–
Civics–Preparation for Naturalization."

As the novel opens, Mr. Kaplan's teacher – the noticeably non-Jewish and quite Protestant Mr. Parkhill (a night school veteran teacher of almost twelve years) – is musing over whether he might have a problem recommending Mr. Kaplan, a lover of learning, for promotion to the next grade (and to a different teacher, Miss Higby) when the current school year is up. However, by the end of the novel Mr. Parkhill is absolutely certain that "by no stretch of the pedagogical imagination" is Mr. Kaplan a candidate for promotion:

> *Mr. Parkhill frowned at the thought of Mr. Kaplan. Mr.*
> *Kaplan was certainly the most energetic and ebullient*
> *pupil. He never missed a lesson; he never grew discouraged;*
> *the smile of undaunted hope and good-will never left his*
> *cherubic face. But, unfortunately, Mr. Kaplan never seemed*
> *to* learn *anything.*

Nevertheless:

> *Mr. Parkhill often wondered whether there wasn't something*
> *sacrilegious in trying to impose the iron mold of English on*
> *so unfettered an intelligence.*

So who is this Mr. Kaplan whose classmates, paradoxically, recognize that he is both the classroom teacher's pest and that same teacher's pet?

Hyman Kaplan is a man in his forties who works full-time during the day (this is night school, remember) as a garment "cotter." By "a cotter" Mr. Kaplan means "a cutter" of cloth in his Yiddish-accented and variable-voweled pronunciation of the job designation for someone who works as a pattern-maker in a dress factory. (Because spoken dialect for the ear and written dialect for the eye do not have the same effect on the human brain, many of the passages in *THE EDUCATION OF HYMAN*

KAPLAN are funnier and smarter and, yes, more joyful, when like the opening pages of *UP THE DOWN STAIRCASE*, they are read aloud.)

Author Leo Rosten has written that dialect humor is "much harder" to write than other forms of humor and "is also more risky, more tricky, more perplexing, and more dangerous":

> *Comic dialect is humor plus anthropology; dialect must seduce the eye to reach the ear and be orchestrated in the brain"; it must tantalize without irritating, and defer without frustrating; it must carry a visual promise to the reader that what he does not instantly recognize can be deciphered with ease and will be rewarded with pleasure; the reader must be cued into making what he thinks is his own special and private discovery – a discovery of delight which, he suspects, neither the character nor the author fully appreciates.*

> *Dialect is not transcription. Nothing is more depressing than a passage of broken English exactly transcribed from the spoken. The "accurate ear" for which a writer is praised is as inventive as it is accurate. It is creative, not literal, for the writer transforms that which he hears into that which you could not. There is a magic in dialect which can liberate us from the prisons of the familiar.*

Sounding out and sounding like Mr. Kaplan can be no easy achievement (as some **Staying After School** students found out from their oral presentations and written projects in "The Teacher and Student in Literature" course). For example, when Hyman Kaplan says "fond mine fife fit don," he is telling us that having lost something, he found it five feet down" (found what was mine five feet down).

Here are three different ways in which Hyman Kaplan creates "amazing renditions of the English language":

- Mr. Kaplan answers that the opposite of "new" is **"second-hand"** instead of "old" (because of his real world clothing background in the garment industry); similarly, **"skinny"** is the logical real world antonym for "rich";

- "verbal indiscretions" were caused for Mr. Kaplan by a **"sleeping of the tong"**; had he pronounced his vowels correctly and knew English grammar better, Mr. Kaplan would have said something closer to "a slip of the tongue" to categorize a faux pas;

- Mr. Kaplan gives the plural of "cat" as **"Katz"** (a familiar Jewish last name spelled that way in writing and too often stereotypically mispronounced as "ketts"); the correct plural is "cats."

Staying After School students and what-if writers came to know and understand Hyman Kaplan as someone who:

- is high-spirited, irrepressible, indomitable – an earnest and enthusiastic "Student" with a capital "S," an adult ed zestful lover of life and learning who signs all his written work with a nine "star-studded" signature in red, blue, and green;

- has only one desire and that is to be the center of attention and impress his teacher, Mr. Parkhill (who "clung with undaunted faith" to the instructional method for his students of "direct participation" and sometimes wondered whether Mr. Kaplan "might not be some sort of genius");

- has a strong sense of himself in competition with the other students in the class, particularly "no soch woid" Mr. Norman Bloom, and "oi!," "poor Mrs. Moskowitz who simply had no ear for sounds," and the "sweet, shy maiden," Miss Rose Mitnick, who was "easily the best student in the class";

- has an ongoing problem of applying his German-sounding Yiddish pronunciation patterns to American English words and phrases, and a separate problem of matching his daily work-in-progress speaking vocabulary with his newly learned correct writing vocabulary; "sometimes Mr. Parkhill thought Mr. Kaplan would never find peace until he had invented a language all his own";

- has a "particular genius" of a mind that can be so idiosyncratically logical that it makes a psychological mess of English grammar, vocabulary, pronunciation, spelling, idioms, you name it (and say it aloud and correctly!); Mr. Kaplan does not deny that the English language has rules – good sensible rules – but he can be this close to conclusive that the rules do not apply to him; referring to his own "dip thinking," Hyman Kaplan will argue that he meant "dip" when he said "dip" (and not "deep," Mr. Parkhill's correction) because students "dip" into their knowledge when they think.

So, "netcherally," **Staying After School** students and what-if writers jumped at the chance to jump to the conclusions of that unique mind and explain Hyman Kaplan – as Hyman Kaplan would inimitably explain himself – with particular reference to Mr. Kaplan's own final written "voids" in the novel about moving on to the next grade of night school with most of his fellow classmates: "I dont care if I don't pass, I *love* the class." **Staying After School** students also responded strongly to the unique "odd couple" bond between continually challenging student Mr. Kaplan and his remarkable teacher **Mr. Parkhill**.

What follows are letters (accented and unaccented!) from Mr. Kaplan (as well as snippets from Mr. Kaplan's personal journal) about that special-with-a-capital-"S" relationship between teacher and student. In every case, the objective of the what-if writers of these pieces was to be humorous (which, you will remember, Leo Rosten defined as "the affectionate communication of insight").

By the way, in a more serious vein, you might consider doing some similar "creative" writing of your own: a "love letter" to a remarkable teacher that you had in middle school, high school, or college. And sending it! Haven't you sometimes thought about doing just that?

Here is **Taylor Fatima** *on and as* Hyman Kaplan:

Hello, Mr. Parkhill!!!

I should telling why I love the class and I dont care if I dont pass. This class by Mr. Parkhill is high class. I making som mistakes, netcheral. Not just class is high class but experience in class is high class. Student like Mitnick, Blum, Moskowitz, Warsaw, and me coming to N.Y. and belonging in school of this is high class.

We tell opinions and hear opinions, and write paper, and write opinion on board, and read opinion from paper, and recite opinion from head and write opinion and thoughts on exam. This is good because coming to N.Y. we are depressed workers of world and are being exploited by bosses who hollers when I am telling shoud be better conditions.

In like, many persons do not listens to mine thoughts and mine opinions. But in high class by Mr. Parkhill I am heard. I get to be star. I get to attention. This making happy for me. Learning and being heard.

So this is why I love the class and do not care if I do not pass. I can retake? No? And have more high class experience.

> *Your animated student,*
> *Affectionately,*

> *H*Y*M*A*N K*A*P*L*A*N*

Here is **Daniel Garcia-Munoz Garcia**, *prosaically and poetically*, on Hyman Kaplan:

> *Dear Mr. Pockheel,*
>
> *I vant to say to you that I love your teachink so much and I learnt a lot. Befor, I didn't know anythink about English and danks to you I now speakink very well. I am a butter man now because of you!*
>
> *As a prisont, I vill like to write a poem, because you know I love poetry, specially shaksbeer:*
>
> *Hello, Mr. Pockheel,*
> *do you know how I feel?*
> *Im very delight,*
> *you taught us to write.*
>
> *I dont care if I dont pass*
> *cause Im stayink in your class.*
> *Im happy to stay with you,*
> *Are you happy too?*
>
> *By H*Y*M*A*N K*A*P*L*A*N*

Here is **Evan Wezik** *on* and *as* Hyman Kaplan:

> *Dear Mr. Parkhill (I hope I slept dis vight),*
>
> *Thank you vor da hard vork you put me through durving dese nights at school. Plizz know dat if I must vepeat da class I vill vork and do mine best. I know I can be odd to teach somteims,*

*but I will do betta and follow da vules. The vules of English
can pozzle me greatly. You of vall peele should know dis. But
the vules of English fancanat me. I enjoyed da assigmants
that ve did in de classes.*

*If I must vepeat the coorse agan I vill be egar to have you teach
me. You are a good leeder. Like Judge Washington or Abram
Lincohen. You alvays chaling us to do hover best. Vemember
when you chose me foist for me to vead my business ladder?
That vas vary nice. Alvough, you told me dat "affectionately"
vas not an appropriate vay to end dat tip of ladder. So I vill
end this von in dat manner since it is personal. I vlokk forwad
to seein you soon.*

Affectionately,
H*Y*M*A*N K*A*P*L*A*N

Here is a non-ethnic-sounding translation of a Mr. Kaplan letter as
created by **Lilly Lin**:

Dear Mr. Parkhill,

*I love this class because it is only during this class where I get to
think I not only like to think but I like to be seen, noticed, heard,
and in general feel that I am an individual, not an anonymous
worker as a cutter toiling away for a boss who doesn't even know
my name. I like the class a lot because I learn, interact, and
question others and I feel even happier when the other students
do the same to me except for maybe Miss Mitnick.*

*Learning a new language is hard but I love to play around
with words – thinking logically – to see how they fit and how*

it can express my feelings. I know I make a lot of mistakes
but isn't that part of being a student, making mistakes and
correcting them or forgetting them and coming back to them?
I love this class so I really don't care if I don't even pass.

*By H*Y*M*A*N K*A*P*L*A*N*

Here is a snippet from Hyman Kaplan's personal journal at the very end of the term as transcribed by **Christine Gargano**:

I was just informed that I would have to repeat English class
at my night school for grown-ups (like me!). I can think
of a few reasons as to why I have to take this course over.
I spell oddly, I pronounce things in a strange way, and I
often misinterpret meanings of words and phrases. I know
some of the other students may find me entertaining, while
others find me to be obnoxious. Mostly, I wonder about Mr.
*P*a*r*k*h*i*l*l, my wonderful teacher who may have been*
confused as to what to do with me.

And here is a different snippet from Hyman Kaplan's personal journal at the very end of the term as transcribed by **Krenare Celaj**:

I am so lucky to have Mr. Parkhill who is extremely patient
with me. He's my favorite person! I don't care that much
about my classmates. I am more focused on impressing Mr.
Parkhill. Hopefully the second time around I can learn and
I can impress my teacher at the same time. More importantly,
let's hope there won't be a third time!

As mentioned earlier in this chapter, the story of Hyman Kaplan didn't end with his initial "education" in 1937. In *THE RETURN OF*

H*Y*M*A*N K*A*P*L*A*N, published by popular demand twenty-two years later in 1959, Rosten wrote his fans, "My thanks go out to all of you...who made this book necessary"; and nine years after that in 1968, a Broadway musical comedy, adapted from both Hyman Kaplan novels, was produced using the first book's title. That mainstage musical comedy – *THE EDUCATION OF H*Y*M*A*N K*A*P*L*A*N* – was directed by the legendary theater director George Abbott and contained fully thirteen original songs, including the immigrant-themed and educationally enlightening "Strange New World," "A Dedicated Teacher," "Anything Is Possible," and "All American."

It closed after 28 performances ("sech a flop!"). No stars.

9

What-if Words of Educational Wisdom: A Class Act Assortment of Acronyms Created in a "Hurry" (Haste Under Rapidly Receding Year)

If this book has a motto (and nineteen **Staying After School** contributors believe that it does), that motto might well be the last instruction in the maxim quoted at the beginning of Chapter 7 – "Involve me, and I understand."

And what better way to conclude a book on the calling of teaching and the answering of learning than through an assortment of educational acronyms created by **Staying After School** students and what-if writers under deadline pressure as our course on "The Teacher and Student in Literature" quickly ran out of days with so much more to teach and learn (it is always thus!).

Enjoy! *E*nter *N*ow *J*auntily *O*r *Y*earn (hopelessly, for time not forthcoming)!

Education

*Everybody Deserves Unique Coaching and Thoughtful
    Individuated Optimistic Nourishment*

*Everything Determining Understanding (Complex and
    Tangled Information Obtained Non-Stop)*

Teach

To Encourage and Challenge Humans

To Educate All Children Harmoniously

Taking Education and Constructing Humanity

Trying to Educate Adolescents Creatively (and) Happily

*Training (in) Excellent Academics (that) Creates
    Happiness*

Try Eagerly and Care Hard

To Empathize and Culturally Humanize

Talking Endlessly About Changing History

True Education: Aim Class High

Learn

Listen Earnestly and Respond Naturally

Listen, Empathize, Absorb, Re-use Naturally

Listening Ears and Ready Noggins

Live Empathetically and Reason Normally

School

Social Congregation Holding Overly Obligated Learners

Several Crucial Hours of Our Lives

Structure Created (to) House Our Ordinary Learners

College

*Classes of Learning Lovers Enthralled Genuinely
    Everyday*

Course
Compilation of Useful Resources (for) Student Education

Class
Collection (of) Learners Acquiring Superlative Scholarship
Creative Lecture and Study Sessions
Classically Learning as Students Sit
Cumulative Lessons and Stimulation (of) Students
Collective Learning About Social Standards
Customary Learning of Arts (and) Social Sciences
Communication Lasting a Single Session

Lesson
Learning Every Single Subject Over-Night

Student
Surviving to Understand Daily – Everyday – Nuances
    Theoretically
Someone Taking (the) Upper-hand (to) Design
    Exceptionally Noteworthy Tomorrows

Pupil
Person Uneducated Possibly Interested (in) Learning

Test / Tests
Torture Every Single Time
To Examine Students That Suffer

Fail
Faux pas (of) Attainable Intelligible Learning
Flat Achievement in Learning

Pass

Perceivable Achievement (through) Success (of) Standards
Positive Achievement Scholastically Speaking

At the start of **Staying After School** (when school was "in"), I wrote:

> *If you are interested in the profession of teaching as a possible*
> *calling or simply intrigued by what goes into good instruction*
> *and real learning (and that "odd couple" relationship of*
> *challenging student and remarkable teacher), this book with*
> *its unusual origins might be the book for you.*

And now, nine chapters later, school is almost "out." My nineteen collaborators and I hope that in "staying after school" with us you have been informed, instructed, and entertained – and that (grading pens, or pencils, at the ready!) you have given our book a passing mark for a "positive achievement scholastically speaking."

Afterward

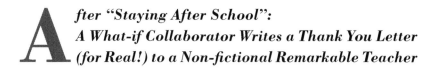

After *"Staying After School":*
A What-if Collaborator Writes a Thank You Letter
(for Real!) to a Non-fictional Remarkable Teacher

Letter to a Remarkable Teacher from a Former Student:

Dear Mr. Fischer,

You were my Intro to College Algebra teacher my junior year of high school. I had heard the class was relatively easy, contrary to the implications of its title. Upon being in the class, I quickly came to realize that the class was NOT as easy as its reputation claimed, and I was quickly filled with worry about my GPA drastically dropping. I always prided myself on being a studious person who cared about my grades and always made an effort to succeed in any assignments or tests. However, I also knew math was not my strong point and that throughout my whole entire youth mathematics had been a concept I never fully grasped.

Being in your class changed that for me. You were so patient and thoughtful with your teaching methods. You realized we, as students, were individuals and that you had to approach each of us with a certain attitude and approach. You realized I was eager to understand the complicated concepts you brought to each lesson and ensured me that through practice and confidence in myself I would succeed.

And that's exactly what happened. I practiced my math every single day, participated in every class, and never felt afraid to ask questions. The class I was most afraid of ruining my GPA ended up being the class I got the highest grade in. I was so proud of myself. You even encouraged me to help other classmates of mine who were struggling in the course. When I did, they also got higher grades and some even ended up being able to graduate because of it.

That was a truly remarkable feeling that I will never forget. It was all because of you. You influenced me in a very strong way and turned my perspective completely around about a topic I never thought I'd understand. And due to that confidence, I pursued many math courses in college and I'm even working part-time at a bank now. That is something I'd never imagine I'd do. Although it may not be my long-term career goal, I found a job I truly love because your class gave me the self-assurance I needed to be able to take chances on certain classes or jobs I never would have considered before.

So, in short, all I want to say is: thank you. You truly do have a strong influence on your students. I know it can be frustrating on your end. Some of us may not be eager to learn. That may be from our own self-doubt. But I know personally you were one of the few teachers I've ever had that never stopped trying. Even when students yelled or got angry or even simply stopped showing interest. Even when you had personal problems with your children's health and had to take some time off to take care of them. Your persistence in your student's well-being and education is what truly shined through. And I will never forget that.

So thank you again. I hope you are well.

Best,

Christine Gargano

Class of 2013

Cast of Characters:
Remarkable Teachers,
Challenging Students

Miss Frizzle *of THE MAGIC SCHOOL BUS series of juvenile novels/*
picture books and pbs television series
Miss Tansy Culver *of THE TEACHER'S FUNERAL, young adult novel*
Miss Jean Brodie *of THE PRIME OF MISS JEAN BRODIE, novel*
"Sir" (E. R. Braithwaite/Mark Thackery)
of TO SIR, WITH LOVE, novel and film
Miss Honey *and* **Miss Trunchbull**
of MATILDA, young adult novel and Broadway musical

Students from Fiction

Gregory Miller *of THE BLACKBOARD JUNGLE, novel,*
and BLACKBOARD JUNGLE, film
Hyman Kaplan *of THE EDUCATION OF HYMAN*
KAPLAN, novel, and THE RETURN OF HYMAN KAPLAN, novel
Angela Adams *of GOOD MORNING, MISS DOVE, novel*
Hamilton Knapp *and* **Jared Lord** *of THE VIEW FROM*
SATURDAY, young adult novel
Joe Ferone *of UP THE DOWN STAIRCASE, novel*
"The Hawk" *of UP THE DOWN STAIRCASE, novel*
Matilda *of MATILDA, young adult novel and Broadway musical*

About the Author

A former journalist, Robert Eidelberg served for nineteen and a half years as the chair of the English Department of William Cullen Bryant High School in New York City and a total of 32 years as a secondary school English teacher in the New York City public school system.

Upon "graduating" from Bryant, a Queens neighborhood high school, Mr. Eidelberg was an educational and editorial consultant and author for Amsco School Publications and a writing instructor at Audrey Cohen Metropolitan College of New York as well as at Queensborough Community College of the City University of New York.

For the past 20 years, Mr Eidelberg has been a college adjunct both supervising undergraduate and graduate student teachers in secondary English education and, on the campus of Brooklyn College of the City University of New York, supervising first-year and second-year probationary teachers in the national Teaching Fellows program. On the campus of Hunter College of the City University of New York, Mr. Eidelberg teaches as an adjunct in the English Department a special topics elective course on "The Teacher and Student in Literature," which he especially created for Hunter College in 2015.

As a working author with a fondness for somewhat lengthy subtitles for his now seven books, Mr. Eidelberg specializes in educational how-to "books with a built-in teacher." *STAYING AFTER SCHOOL* is a 19-student co-authored companion book to Mr. Eidelberg's 2013 career and instructional text *SO YOU THINK YOU MIGHT LIKE TO TEACH*. Along with his life partner of forty-four years and their Whippet, Chandler, Robert Eidelberg lives in the Park Slope neighborhood of Brooklyn, New York.

Made in the USA
Middletown, DE
18 May 2020

95323070R00076